# To Blind the Eyes of Our Enemies
## Washington's Grand Deception

Copyright ©2018 G.L. Lamborn & W.L. Simpson, Jr.

Library of Congress Cataloging-in-Publication Data
Lamborn, G.L. and Simpson, W.L., Jr.
*To Blind the Eyes of Our Enemies: Washington's Grand Deception*

Library of Congress Control Number: 2018937831
ISBN: 978-1-942923-31-2

# TO BLIND THE EYES OF OUR ENEMIES
## WASHINGTON'S GRAND DECEPTION

G.L. LAMBORN

W.L. SIMPSON, JR.

# Dedication

We dedicate this book to the American secret agents of the Revolutionary War without whose courageous and skillful efforts in helping to blind the eyes of our enemies under Washington's guiding hand, American independence could not have been won.

This volume is also dedicated to the Sons of the American Revolution (SAR) and the Daughters of the American Revolution (DAR) in support of their work to promote better understanding of the meaning of the American Revolution and the formation of our identity as a nation.

# Acknowledgments

The authors wish to express their gratitude to the following individuals for their encouragement, support, and valuable historical insights: Walter Jervis Sheffield, Esq., Rick Pinzon, Mike Schaefer, Lt. George Wisnieski, USN, Lt. Col. Peter Badger, USMC (Ret.), Hon. W. Page Johnson II, and Larry McKinley. Their contributions and encouragement made this tribute to George Washington's genius possible.

# Contents

| | |
|---|---|
| I - Practice to Deceive | 9 |
| II - A Second Fabius | 17 |
| III - Hanging in the Balance | 23 |
| IV - "Such an Army, So Well Appointed" | 33 |
| V - Glory and Danger Alike | 43 |
| VI - Flying on "Canvas Wings" | 49 |
| VII - Allies and Traitors | 63 |
| VIII - Point of Decision: North or South? | 72 |
| IX - Washington's Confession | 84 |
| X - Washington's Sound and Light Show | 94 |
| XI - Washington's Boffo Performance | 100 |
| XII - The Great Mailbag Caper | 111 |
| XIII - End of the Southern Campaign | 133 |
| XIV - In Quest of Adventure | 140 |
| XV - Their Lordships Confer | 147 |
| XVI - White Flag over Yorktown | 159 |
| XVII - Epilogue | 169 |
| Bibliography | 173 |
| The Americans | 179 |
| The British | 183 |
| The French | 191 |
| British Forces in America | 200 |
| Author Biographies | 202 |

# I

## Practice to Deceive

> If I shall be able to rise superior to these and many other difficulties, which might be enumerated, I shall most religiously believe, that the finger of Providence is in it, to blind the eyes of our enemies; for surely if we get well through this month, it must be for want of their knowing the disadvantages we labour under.
>
> George Washington
> Letter to Joseph Reed
> 14 January 1776

George Washington, the architect of American independence, was a man blessed with genius that was clothed in his modesty, quiet dignity, discretion and infallible courtesy. Historians generally concur that Washington was "the indispensable man" in winning the American Revolution and securing liberty to the Thirteen Colonies. While historians recognize his leadership during even the darkest periods of the Revolutionary War, many do not fully appreciate the depth of Washington's genius as a general and as a grand strategist.

Genius is that rare combination of vision and imagination that enables a man to see what others cannot see and grasp instantly not merely the significance of what has been seen, but also conceive what must be done.

Conventional historical writing has it that Washington was slow to understand the British strategic vulnerability in America – with major forces divided between the defense of New York City and the occupation of the American South. Many historians claim that it was only in mid-August 1781 at the urging of the sagacious Comte de Rochambeau that Washington *finally* comprehended that he could decisively defeat Cornwallis by concentrating land forces and sea power around the British defenses at Yorktown. This school of historians holds that only at the last moment – and then begrudgingly – did Washington give up his long held dream of laying siege to New York and inflicting a defeat on the British there. Many believe that the French forced Washington's hand, very much against his will, thereby compelling him to focus upon Yorktown.

In support of their view these historians tally up voluminous correspondence, documents, and other commentary by Washington stating that the British stronghold of New York City was his single-minded target until 14 August 1781.

Most historians recognize George Washington as a man of courage and integrity. However, what many of his biographers have failed to recognize is Washington's matchless grasp of the strategic and political factors essential to victory – and his own clear realization after November 1776 of his perpetual military weakness. They thus short-change Washington's vision and intelligence and rob him of his true greatness.

Washington may well be the nation's most underrated general.

Historians debate Washington's skills as a field commander. His detractors point out his many defeats – especially those at New York in 1776 and around Philadelphia in 1777. While it may be true that Washington was merely the equal of his British foes tactically, with a mixed dance card of defeats and victories, his tactical masterpiece in December 1776 at Trenton and Princeton suggests that he had considerable tactical skill.[1] But whatever Washington's merits as a tactician, *as a strategist he had no peer on either side.*

The foundation for his strategic vision and genius for war was George Washington's mastery of intelligence collection and deception operations. It was Washington's talent for secrecy and deception that was critical to ultimate victory over the British and to securing unconditional American independence at Yorktown.

> I believe I may with great truth affirm that no man perhaps since the first institution of armies ever commanded one under more difficult circumstances than I have done. To enumerate the particulars would fill a volume. *Many of the difficulties and distresses were of so peculiar a cast that, in order to conceal them from the enemy, I was obliged to conceal them from my friends, and indeed from my own army, thereby subjecting my conduct to interpretations unfavorable to my character, especially by those at a distance who could not in the smallest degree be acquainted with the springs that governed it.*[2]

Strategic deceptions are enormously difficult to conceptualize and even more difficult to bring off successfully. The challenge facing a planner is to anticipate every detail and meticulously prepare a picture of operations that, although false, has the absolute ring of truth to his opponent.

Deception is not merely simulating a few tanks or gun emplacements. That will fool no one. Instead, a successful deception begins on a far deeper level. It begins with deep understanding of

---

1 No less a figure than Frederick the Great marveled at Washington's tactical brilliance at Trenton and Princeton. (Dupuy, p. 712) The Trenton campaign probably saved the faltering American Revolution. Washington used the double agent, John Honeyman, to convince Colonel Johannes Rall that no American attack was imminent. (Bakeless, p. 169)

2 George Washington letter to John Augustine Washington, 31 March 1776. (PGW: R, Vol. 3, pp. 566-70) Italics added for emphasis.

the mind and psychology of the enemy commander and his staff. More, it must comprehend his thinking style, the means by which he gathers and appraises raw information, makes his assumptions, and arrives at conclusions. In short, the planner who would dupe his enemy not only must have clear understanding of his foe's decision-making process, but also the means to manipulate that process.

In more recent history, the best example we have of a successful strategic deception is the "First U.S. Army Group" (or FUSAG) deception in early 1944 used to mask Overlord, the Allied landings on the Normandy coast.[3] In formulating the great cover plan for Overlord, the key to success lay in analyzing and thoroughly comprehending Hitler's assumptions about Allied intentions. The Fuhrer had certain fixed views about what the Anglo-American commanders would do and what they would not do. In addition, Hitler and the High Command (OKW) had intelligence resources that they used to monitor Allied preparations and capabilities. The challenge for the British and American officers who planned the deception was to reinforce views already held by Hitler and the OKW about a main landing in the Pas de Calais. To do this, the Allies created a totally fictitious unit – the FUSAG – and orchestrated all Allied activities to give Hitler's spies and technical intelligence collectors the "evidence" they sought "confirming" the Fuhrer's intuition about the location and nature of the cross-Channel invasion that everyone on both sides knew was coming.

As is well known, the FUSAG deception worked so well that it was not until July that Hitler finally gave permission to re-deploy the German Fifteenth Army in an attempt to stop the Anglo-American offensive (and save the remnants of the by-now mauled Seventh Army.) But by then, it was far too late; the deception had

---

3 Known to the Allied planners as "Plan Jael" after the Israelite woman who killed the Canaanite general Sisera by first lulling him into a false sense of security. (see Judges 4: 17-24) (Weigley, p. 113)

succeeded. The Allies were well on their way to Paris, and ultimately to the Rhine.

Strategic deception has played its part in warfare since the time of Sun Tzu in the fifth century B.C. when Master Sun observed that: "All warfare is based upon deception."

> Therefore, when capable, feign incapacity; when active, inactivity. When near, make it appear that you are far away; when far away, that you are near. Offer the enemy a bait to lure him; feign disorder and strike him.[4]

During World War I Winston Churchill reflected on the senseless carnage brought about by the head-butting of trench warfare and wrote:

> There is required for the composition of a great commander not only massive common sense and reasoning power, not only imagination, but also an element of legerdemain, an original and sinister touch, which leaves the enemy puzzled as well as beaten…[5]

Shortly before the Tehran Conference of late 1943, when planning for Overlord was well underway, and all involved well knew the high risk of the assault and the poor odds of success, Churchill made a comment that has become iconic:

> In war-time, truth is so precious that she should always be attended by a bodyguard of lies.[6]

---

4 Sun Tzu, The Art of War, p. 66; Samuel Griffith, trans. On succeeding pages, additional guidance is given: "Keep him [enemy] under a strain and wear him down. When he is united, divide him. Attack where he is unprepared; sally out when he does not expect you."

5 Brown, Bodyguard of Lies, p. 5

6 ibid, p. 10

Successful deception operations are built around two seemingly incompatible conditions: revealing to the enemy 90 percent of what he wishes to see – basically the truth – while concealing the vital 10 percent that must be hidden. In a sense, it is playing a gigantic confidence game for the highest of stakes, basing that game not on the *stupidity* of the "mark," but on his *acumen*. It assumes a vigilant and experienced enemy. But it also plays upon his preconceived or unconscious notions, his prejudices, and his ego.

The planner of a deception must figuratively "see the world as the enemy sees it" and put himself in his opponent's shoes. *If I were the intelligence officer of my enemy's army, what would I most want to know? Where should I look? Whom should I question? What do I expect to find? How will I "know it when I see it?"*

But even those are merely starting points. One veteran intelligence officer described his profession as a "wilderness of mirrors." A clever intelligence officer is constantly on the lookout for deception. Indeed, he *expects* to be deceived. Veteran intelligence officers always regard raw reports with healthy – and well-deserved – skepticism. Addressing this problem, Karl von Clausewitz noted that:

> A great part of the information obtained in war is contradictory, a still greater part false, and by far the greatest part somewhat doubtful. What is required of an officer in this case is a certain power of discrimination, which only knowledge of men and things and good judgment can give. The law of probability must be his guide.[7]

And yet, as we know from the FUSAG deception of 1944, and other past deceptions going back to the legendary Trojan Horse, despite careful analytical work and healthy skepticism, even the experienced and the wise can be gulled. How can this be?

---

7 Clausewitz, <u>On War</u>, Book I, Chapter 6, p. 117

Perhaps the heart of the matter is *expectation*. As human beings we make certain basic assumptions about the world we live in, about ourselves and our actions, and about the people around us – both friends and enemies. Based upon our experience, we *expect* certain things to happen. Most often *we expect a continuation – more or less – of familiar, established patterns of activity*. Few people expect that each new day will be radically unlike all other days that have preceded it. This leads us over time to form certain habits in our expectations about what *will* happen. If what we observe in the world consistently conforms to our expectations, then our behavioral patterns and assumptions are steadily reinforced. At a certain point, when our assumptions have been proved correct time after time, and have taken on the nature of a fixed or ingrained habit, we cease to take seriously information that tends to conflict with our expectations. At that point, we blind ourselves to the possibility that future events may not be as we expect them to be. We thereby render ourselves vulnerable to surprise.

When patterns of thought become unconsciously ingrained, we tend to see only what confirms these familiar patterns. Indeed, it is literally possible to "not see" anomalies. They are filtered out from our consciousness.[8] Few people routinely question their assumptions by asking themselves: *"but what if my assumptions are wrong?"* And few people are observant enough to "see all there is to

---

[8] In a famous experiment concerning cognition, observers were asked to watch closely and count the number of times a basketball was tossed between six or seven players. As the ball was being tossed to and fro, a man dressed in a gorilla suit walked in clear view behind the players. Despite his obvious presence, less than half of those who had been closely observing the players toss the ball even noticed the "gorilla." Psychologists concluded that many observers had been so intent on watching the ball being tossed to and fro that they had mentally "locked out" anomalies such as the unexpected "gorilla." See Daniel J. Simons and Christopher F. Chabris, "Gorillas in our midst: sustained inattentional blindness for dynamic events," Perception, Vol. 28, pp. 1059-74; Harvard University, 1999.

see." Sir Arthur Conan Doyle's character, Sherlock Holmes, once chided his faithful associate, Dr. Watson, by saying that he had seen, but failed to *observe*.[9]

The Nobel laureate economist Friedrich Hayek once stated that: *"Never will a man penetrate deeper into error than when he is continuing on a road that has led him to great success."*[10] A strategy built upon habitual conventional thinking, especially when that thinking is reinforced by prejudice or illusion, will lead only to disaster – a truth that Sir Henry Clinton learned the hard way from his American service.

---

9 Line from Sir Arthur Conan Doyle's novel <u>A Scandal in Bohemia</u>. The exact quotation is: "You have not observed. And yet you have seen."

10 Friedrich Hayek, <u>Counterrevolution of Science: Studies on the Abuse of Reason</u>, p. 175.

# II

# A Second Fabius

The great general Hannibal posed an existential threat to Carthage's national enemy, Rome. As is well known, Hannibal crossed the Alps in Fall 218 B.C. to attack Roman power on its home ground, Italy. Once in Italy, Hannibal proved himself time and again to be one of history's greatest generals. All Roman generals who dared to oppose him in open battle were defeated – at Trebia, Lake Trasimenus, and ultimately at the greatest Roman disaster of all time, at Cannae.

There was only one general who was equal to Hannibal. This was Quintus Fabius Maximus Varrucosus, known to history as Fabius Maximus "Cunctator," The Delayer.

Fabius Maximus knew that in open battle Hannibal was certain to sweep all before him. Indeed, at Cannae alone, on 2 August 216 B.C., Rome lost 60,000 men. A few more such defeats and Rome itself would collapse, and with its defeat Italy and the Mediterranean would pass under Carthaginian rule.

Fabius thereupon developed a strategy for limiting Hannibal's operations in Italy by ensuring that Rome always maintained a "force in being," but never risked that force in open battle. Rather, Fabius would maneuver against the Carthaginians, but stay just out of Hannibal's reach. Fabius believed that time and distance would gradually wear down his enemy, and that sooner or later logistical realities and lack of manpower would force Hannibal to leave Italy. All that was required, thought Fabius, was to outlast the enemy while conserving Roman strength.

Many of his fellow Romans did not see things the way Fabius did. They desired frontal attacks on the main Carthaginian army that would result in its decisive defeat in the field. Some Romans considered Fabius to be either a coward or an incompetent. Not a few Roman leaders heaped abuse or ridicule on Fabius for his lack of decisive "results." Fabius bore these insults with dignity and forbearance. The historian Plutarch quotes Fabius as saying:

> "In that case, surely," said he, "I should be a greater coward than I am now held to be, if through fear of abusive jests I should abandon my fixed plans. And verily the fear which one exercises in behalf of his country is not shameful; but to be frightened from one's course by the opinions of men, and by their slanderous censures, that marks a man unworthy of so high an office as this, who makes himself the slave of the fools over whom he is in duty bound to be lord and master."[1]

Ultimately, Fabian strategy proved not merely wise but successful. The Roman republic preserved itself despite fifteen years of defensive war against Hannibal. In large measure, it was thanks to Fabius Maximus that Rome survived.

When viewing Washington from the perspective of Time as a "second Fabius" we see his prudence and good judgment. Many of his critics at the time saw undue hesitation and incompetence. The historian Joseph Ellis describes George Washington's natural inclination as proactive, taking the initiative, and striving for a quick decision. Washington was not the kind of man who waited for others to act, but preferred to take action. Ellis goes on to say that George Washington believed that the "honorable" soldier met his opponent in open battle and relied upon his courage and virtue

---

1 Plutarch, <u>Lives</u>: Quintus Fabius Maximus Cunctator.

to carry the day. His conception of war, perhaps typical of his Age, was that of a chivalrous duel fought openly, man-to-man.²

Insurgencies, however, are fought between *unequals* – most normally between a strong occupying power having a well-equipped army, and a weak shadow government and its poorly trained and ill-equipped armed element. In the case of the American Revolution, the British government held nearly all the tangible advantages – it had money, thousands of trained soldiers, the world's most powerful navy, and an established political structure. By contrast, the American insurgents had none of these advantages. Even the idea of "independence" was not so deeply held as to induce the majority of American colonists to give up their status as "subjects" to become loyal and active "citizens."

If the Americans were to achieve success in their war for independence, it was clear that they would have to follow a strategy that diminished or offset the advantages enjoyed by the British. In the first two years of the Revolution, the Americans in general, and Washington in particular, learned hard lessons at the hands of the British. One of these was that farmers and tradesmen acting as militia were incapable of meeting highly disciplined British regular troops on an equal footing. Open battles between unequals were certain to result in defeats – perhaps even in a catastrophic defeat from which no recovery was possible.

Perhaps the hardest lesson learned – the Moment of Enlightenment – came with the loss of New York City in the fall of 1776, specifically with the British capture of Fort Washington in November.³ American troop losses on Long Island and Manhattan

---

2 Joseph J. Ellis, <u>His Excellency George Washington</u>. See Chapter Three "First in War."

3 Greene had urged Washington to defend Fort Washington "at all costs." Its fall on 16 November 1776 resulted in the capture of 2,800 badly needed American soldiers and completed the British conquest of New York City. The remnants of the American army straggled across New Jersey to Pennsylvania. See George Washington's letter to John

were staggering. But perhaps the most significant damage to the American cause resulting from the British seizure of New York was psychological. It was now perfectly clear that the soldierly courage of "embattled farmers" and the virtuous cause of American independence would not be enough to ensure victory over British power. On top of this, the colonists' support for independence sank to a low ebb.

The first to learn the hard lesson of inequality appears to have been Nathanael Greene. From the loss of Fort Washington until the end of the war, Greene advised Washington to pursue a cautious "Fabian" strategy. At times Greene had to exhort and admonish his chief not to be *"frightened from one's course by the opinions of men, [or] by their slanderous censures"* and thus goaded into plunging into a head-to-head battle that would surely result in the total destruction of the American army.[4]

Greene also took his own advice, admirably demonstrated during his brilliant southern campaign of 1780-1781 first against Lord Cornwallis and later, against Lord Rawdon.

---

Augustine Washington, 6 Nov 1776. WGW: Fk, Vol. 6, pages 242, 244-5. Washington was mortified at the loss as he had conceived holding the fort to be dangerous since British ships controlled the Hudson. He thought the capture of Fort Washington was important to General Howe, as he otherwise *"would have found it difficult unless some Southern Expedition may prove successful, to have reconciled the People of England to the conquest of a few pitiful islands, none of wch were defensible, considering the great number of their Ships and the power they have by Sea to surround and render them unapproachable."*
This excerpt clearly shows Washington's thinking five years before the Yorktown campaign. Greene never again advocated static defenses or pitched battles against British regulars.

4 Ellis, p. 107. "Greene tried to remind [Washington] that he really had no choice: *'your Excellency has the choice of but two things,'* Greene advised, *'to fight the Enemy without the least Prospect of Success…or remain inactive, & be the subject of Censure of an ignorant & impatient populace.'* Knox chimed in with the same opinion…"

Washington became a "Fabian" only with difficulty and reluctance. His character urged him to openly fight General Howe and later General Clinton. But Washington's hard experience and intellect worked to restrain his combative instincts, since he knew that what the British commanders most desired was a decisive battle in which their greatly superior firepower and tactical discipline would utterly destroy his weaker force.

But even more than his use of a Fabian strategy to wear down British power from Valley Forge until the end of the Revolution, Washington's new persona radiated the reassuring tone of the ancient Roman commander. Plutarch's description of Fabius Maximus perfectly fits the George Washington of Valley Forge and the American Revolution:

> But all were brought at last to be of one mind, namely, that the situation demanded a sole and absolute authority, which they call a dictatorship, and a man who would wield this authority with energy and without fear; that Fabius Maximus, and he alone, was such a man, having a spirit and a dignity of hand that fully matched the greatness of the office, and being moreover at the time of life when bodily vigour still suffices to carry out the counsels of the mind, and courage is tempered with prudence. . . . For he who, in times of apparent security, appeared cautious and irresolute, then, when all were plunged in boundless grief and helpless confusion, was the only man to walk the city with calm step, composed countenance, and gracious address, checking effeminate lamentation, and preventing those from assembling together who were eager to make public their common complaints. He persuaded the senate to convene, heartened up the magistrates, and was himself the strength and power of every magistracy, since all looked to him for guidance.[5]

---

5 Plutarch, Lives: Fabius Maximus Cunctator.

George Washington faced much the same kind of criticisms, whispering campaigns, and actual plots against his leadership as did Fabius Maximus centuries earlier. But the last word concerning both of these reluctant heroes was spoken two millennia ago by Plutarch: *"So Fabius endured the situation calmly and easily, so far as it affected himself, thereby confirming the axiom of philosophy that a sincerely good man can neither be insulted nor dishonoured."*

Washington wrote the following to the President of Congress in fall 1776: *"There is nothing that gives a man consequence, and renders him fit for command, like a support that renders him independent of everybody but the State he serves."*[6] Washington combined in his person both the military and civil traits that were to carry on the American War of Independence to its conclusion at the Peace of Paris of 1783. In no small measure, Washington's success was due to his ability to become a second Fabius.

---

6 George Washington's letter to John Hancock, then President of Congress, 24 September 1776, from Harlem Heights. PGW: R, Vol. 6, pages 393, 395.

# III

# Hanging in the Balance

Central to the outcome of the American Revolution was a kind of mental duel between the two protagonists of the last phase of the war, George Washington and Sir Henry Clinton. The supreme commanders also faced each other through their deputies in the struggle for the South in 1780-81: Nathanael Greene and Lord Charles Cornwallis.

By 1780, after five years of war, both sides were aware that the struggle in America was nearing a decision point. What remained undecided was when that point would be reached, where, and with what outcome. Supreme Commander Sir Henry Clinton still held out a thin hope that Washington would oppose him in an open battle in the North during which British firepower and numbers would decisively smash the Continental Army. But Sir Henry also knew that such a decisive battle was unlikely.

By 1780 Washington was too clever by far to be drawn into a pitched battle with British regulars. But brilliant strategist and master of deception that he was, Washington kept Sir Henry guessing as to what the Americans might do next. Would the Americans attempt a siege against the British stronghold in New York? If so, when? But if not, what then?

Washington's greatness as a strategist rests upon his clear understanding of three key factors that were decisive to his struggle and his uncanny ability to make excellent use of these factors. Washington was always painfully aware of his constant military weakness – dependent as he was on militia levies and the uncertain largesse of the individual state legislatures. He stood in awe of British strategic mobility made possible by the Royal Navy's command of the sea. Above all, Washington intuitively understood the politics of the situation – the mood of his own people and the mind and will of his British enemies.

Recognizing his military weakness, after 1777 Washington never made the mistake of exceeding his meager physical and human resources. Instead, he realized that an "army in being" – even if repeatedly whipped and chased about by his superior foes – was the vital element in keeping America's revolutionary hopes alive. Washington did all in his power to conserve his limited military forces while ceaselessly cajoling Congress, the legislatures and key individuals to help build American strength.

The crippling impact on Washington's strategy imposed by lack of physical resources such as troops, military equipment, and money, is laid bare in his October 1780 response to Lafayette. Responding to a question posed by Lafayette on behalf of the French Court concerning his supposed inactivity, the supreme commander replied:

> It is impossible, my dear Marquis, to desire more ardently than I do to terminate the campaign by some happy stroke; *but we must consult our means rather than our wishes,* and not endeavor to better our affairs by attempting things, which for want of success may make them worse.[1]

---

1 Hughes, p. 584, quoting Washington's letter to Lafayette, 30 October 1780, WGW: Fk, Vol. 20, pages 266-7. See also Ford, <u>Writings</u>, IX, p. 17. Italics added for emphasis; the classic definition of strategy is: "the relationship of means available to the ends sought." This excerpt amply

Although he was never a sailor, it is undeniable that Washington admired the Royal Navy for its capabilities. He was less concerned with the Royal Navy's heavy guns – he would never face them – but was ever mindful of the Navy's almost magical ability to transport and land British forces at will. Washington referred in awe to the Royal Navy as the "canvas wings" of the British army.[2]

Washington's understanding of the critical importance of seapower as an element of strategy is clear from a comment made to Lafayette: *"Without a decisive naval force we can do nothing definitive. And with it, everything honorable and glorious."*[3]

Last, but far from least, Washington always kept himself very well informed of attitudes and events as close by as Morristown and Long Island, or as distant as Martinique and London. But beyond being keenly aware of public opinion and political or military activity, Washington surprisingly often was able to manipulate both politics and public opinion to his advantage. Certainly by 1780, and more likely by the end of the terrible winter at Valley Forge, Washington had become to American Patriots the living symbol of the Revolution and of independence. Large crowds turned out to see him and even (literally) sing his praises.

Washington knew that his struggle was in effect a "people's war" and that it would be decided not merely by military maneuver, but

---

    demonstrates Washington's clear understanding of his limitations, hence his mastery of strategy.

2 As a young man, George Washington had wished to join the Royal Navy, but was prevented by his mother from so doing. We may speculate on the historical consequences for America had he joined the Royal Navy, eventually becoming Admiral Sir George Washington, R.N. We are in his mother's debt. See Chernow, pages 17-18. Also see display on this subject at Mount Vernon.

3 George Washington's letter to Marquis de Lafayette, 15 November 1781; WGW: Fk, Vol. 23, pp. 340-1.

by public opinion. On 13 March 1781, amidst admiring Patriot crowds in New England, Washington told the Comte de Dumas: *"We may be beaten by the English; it is the chance of war; but here is the army that they will never conquer."*[4] Washington was referring to the American people, and especially to its youth. Washington perhaps thought that, even if he should be defeated, American independence would inevitably be achieved by the next generation.

Not least, among the Whigs in Parliament, Washington was viewed with respect as an honorable opponent, and the American cause that he represented was considered by many to be just. Washington's stature at home and abroad grew with each passing year.

Washington undoubtedly knew that America had many friends in Parliament, to include Charles Watson-Wentworth, 2nd Marquess of Rockingham who, as Prime Minister after Grenville, had repealed the Stamp Act. Rockingham would again become Prime Minister after Lord North's fall, and immediately open peace negotiations with America. Other friends in Parliament included the fiery Colonel Isaac Barre, a protégé of Lord Shelburne, who answered Charles Townshend in Parliament on 11 February 1765: *"And believe me, remember I this Day told you so, that same Spirit of Freedom which actuated that people [the Americans] at first, will*

---

4 Hughes, p. 621. Count Dumas recorded the following: *"The whole population had assembled from the suburbs; we were surrounded by a crowd of children carrying torches, reiterating the acclamations of the citizens; all were eager to approach the person of him whom they called their father, and pressed so closely around us that they hindered us from proceeding. General Washington was much affected, stopped a few moments and pressing my hand said, 'We may be beaten by the English; it is the chance of war; but behold an army which they can never conquer.'"* See http://www.quahog.org/factsfolklore/index.php?id=156

*accompany them still."* [5] Although America's friends in Parliament were in the minority [Loyal Opposition] until 1782, they kept up a drumbeat against the war party supporting Lord North, finally ousting North through a vote of "No Confidence" several months after Yorktown.

No British general serving in America had anywhere near Washington's charisma, none were as well informed, and few had his clear grasp of the military reality. It is possible that Sir Henry Clinton alone among the British commanders recognized the vital role of the Royal Navy in providing strategic mobility, and only the Howe brothers could be said to comprehend American attitudes toward the political issues of the day thanks to their own service in America (and that of their brother) during the French and Indian War.

For victory and independence to be won, Washington recognized that three conditions must exist. First, the British must not be permitted to snuff out organized American resistance – the local militias and the weak Continental Army. So long as these forces existed, however weak or tattered, the British would be unable to protect their civil officials from expulsion or ensure British rule where it was challenged. An insurgent master, Washington knew that while tactical victory was desirable, it was not necessary. All that was required for an eventual political settlement with Great Britain was for Washington to avoid being ruined in a disastrous open battle. He knew that time, mounting costs, and frustration

---

5 Jared Ingersoll's letter to Thomas Fitch, 11 February 1765, reporting Barre's speech in Parliament. See http://www.pasleybrothers.com/mocourses/texts/Barre.htm. Barre's speech is well worth reading in its entirety. He castigates the ministry for its blind folly. Barre had served under General Wolfe at Quebec and was well acquainted with the American colonies.

eventually would wear down his British adversaries if only he could find the troops and financial means to persevere.[6]

Along with the need merely to survive while wearing down both the strength and will of his opponents, Washington also recognized that keeping enemy forces divided was vital. Wherever the British were divided, in both their armies and their counsels, it became possible for Washington – even with his weaker forces – to fall upon a part of the British force and defeat or even destroy it. Isolated units, units withdrawing from the battlefield, and those "caught napping" were favorite targets. Thus, far from driving the British out of the major cities they had captured – which would compel them to concentrate their forces – it was imperative to allow as many British garrisons as possible to exist. For each stronghold required a garrison, thereby dispersing British forces over the land in defensive positions where they could be of only tactical, not strategic value. So long as the British forces remained in garrisons – static defenses – they could pose little threat to the consolidation of republican rule in the colonies. Only if the British formed effective maneuver units capable of evicting rebel forces and civil authorities would they pose a dire threat to American independence.

Second, Washington knew that a final victory over his British enemies was unlikely unless the Royal Navy's wings could be clipped. The Continental Navy, and later the swarm of American privateers, clearly was not the tool for this job. While these weak forces could prey on British commerce, they were incapable of blocking His Majesty's ships-of-the-line escorting troop transport ships anywhere along the Atlantic seaboard. What was required, therefore, was to "borrow" a navy from some other naval power. And that implied winning the active support of France or Spain, not merely in symbolic form such as recognition of American

---

6 Indeed, from Valley Forge to the end of the war, Washington considered that the dissolution of his army was more likely from lack of proper support by Congress and the state legislatures than by British attack.

independence, but more concretely by applying naval power at a critical point and time.

British historian Captain W. M. James, C.B, Royal Navy, wrote that:

> Yorktown has often been described as one of the 'decisive battles of the world,' but it was the naval skirmish off the Chesapeake that was decisive….Cornwallis may have been too impetuous, Clinton may have been weak in not giving definite orders to Cornwallis, Germain may have been more wrong-headed than ever, but, allowing all that, the victory in the end was to the holder of the sea line of communications. *From the day Clinton divided his forces on the American seaboard the success of the campaign depended on the sea forces.* [7]

Third, Washington fully understood that sitting in the British Parliament were figures like Burke, Fox, Barre and others who opposed Britain's war in America and advocated negotiations. This being the case, Washington knew that he had two options available to help strengthen his friends' hands in Parliament. If Sir Henry Clinton dithered and delayed with no demonstrable prospect of ever decisively defeating the Americans, it would be clear that the British command itself was prolonging the war at increasing cost in lives, treasure, and lost territory. Parliament was only too well aware that taxpayers at home would bear the costs of the war in America.[8]

---

7 Hughes, p. 655, quoting Captain W.M. James, RN, The Naval History of Great Britain, Vol. 1, 1793-1796; five volumes, 1822-1824, reprinted in six volumes, 1826. Italics added for emphasis.

8 According to Merrill Jensen, <u>The Founding of a Nation: A History of the American Revolution 1763 – 1776</u>, p. 379, the British spent £80 million Sterling on the war which created a national debt of £250 million that it financed at roughly 4% interest. The U.S. Congress spent $37 million with the individual states spending an additional $114 million – mainly

Conversely, if the British were to make the mistake of leaving a large force exposed in an isolated, vulnerable position, Washington could pounce on that force and destroy it even with such forces as he had. Either way, Lord North's many opponents in Parliament could then engineer a "No Confidence" vote – ousting his government from power – and seat a new administration that would open peace negotiations.[9]

Indeed, by 1780 British public discontent was increasing over the American war and other issues. The violent Gordon Riots that rocked London in the summer of 1780, and calls for reduction of royal power, did not go unnoticed in Parliament. Historian Barbara Tuchman noted the following strains in British political life caused by popular discontent and Parliamentary doubts:

> While Parliament and public grew increasingly sour on the war, the King [George III] persisted in its continuance partly because he believed the loss of empire would bring shame and ruin, and more because he could not live with the thought that it would be *his* reign that would forever bear the stigma of the loss.[10]

Sustaining American public opinion was equally important. By 1780 there were enough "Americans" in New England and the

---

raised through loans and the printing of paper currency. France spent 1.3 billion Livres (equivalent to £56 million) thereby creating a national debt of £187 million that it could not easily finance – debt service amounted to more than half of France's annual tax revenue. See also http://www.answers.com/topic/american-revolutionary-war#costs_of_the_war

9 There were at least seven attempts to unseat Lord North by votes of "No Confidence" from November 1781 until his resignation in March 1782 when Parliament finally decided he should go. Lord North had unwisely requested a large sum for the purpose of continuing the American war. Tuchman, pp. 227-228.

10 Tuchman, March of Folly, p. 225. Italics are Tuchman's.

Middle Atlantic colonies to ensure that these two regions would not clamor for restoration of British rule there.[11] But was the same true of the southern colonies, to include the Old Dominion of Virginia? Washington was fully aware of the economic realities of the South – an agrarian region dependent on exporting cash crops such as cotton and tobacco – and the pro-British sympathies of many colonists in the Carolinas and Georgia. What would be the political consequences of a *third* crushing American defeat on top of those suffered in Charleston in May 1780 and at Camden in August?

But if the British expeditionary forces could be trapped and starved into submission – or destroyed outright – what then would be the impact on public opinion in the South?

Fully cognizant of the political and military realities of victory or defeat, Washington knew by the summer of 1780 that the issue of full national independence – not merely a limited and conditional independence of *part* of the United States as proffered in 1778 by the Carlisle peace delegation – rejected by the Continental Congress – was hanging in the balance.[12] Until late September 1780 and his first meeting with the French commanders at Hartford, Connecticut,

---

11 This is not to ignore important pockets of Loyalists in Pennsylvania, Maryland, and New York, but to point out that by 1780 republican legislatures were firmly established in the north and that Tory groups there had become politically irrelevant without a permanent British military presence.

12 Washington's position on total independence is clear from his letter of 21 April 1778 to John Bannister, then at Carlisle, Pennsylvania: *"Nothing short of independence, it appears to me, can possibly do. A peace on other terms would, if I may be allowed the expression, be a peace of war. ... France, by her supplies, has saved us from the yoke thus far; and a wise and virtuous perseverance would, and I trust will, free us entirely."* WGW: Fk, Vol. 11, pages 284, 290. Upon Sir William Howe's capture of Philadelphia after the Battle of Brandywine, Congress had evacuated to Carlisle.

Washington believed that final victory would be won at New York. But after his painstaking re-appraisal of strategic realities and the limits to his naval and military capabilities, Washington concluded that the ultimate decision would instead be made somewhere in the South.

# IV

# "Such an Army, So Well Appointed"

The flags dipped in salute as General Sir William Howe, His Majesty's commander-in-chief in America, relinquished his command in May 1778 and stepped aboard a British warship bound for Portsmouth. General Howe and his brother, Admiral Lord Richard Howe, returned to face a firestorm of criticism for their conduct of the American war. General Howe was pilloried in the press and in Parliament for his handling of British forces during the disastrous Saratoga campaign of 1777, his failure to destroy Washington's army in 1776, and the allegation that he was "too lenient" on the rebellious colonists throughout his tenure. Howe's critics demanded to know why:

> ... Such an army, so well appointed, served by so large a train of artillery, and attended by so numerous a fleet, could fail of success against a divided people, destitute of Officers, Soldiers, Magazines, fortified towns, ships of war, or any apparent resources.[1]

---

1 Billias, p.40, quoting *"A View of the Evidence relative to the Conduct of the American War"* published anonymously in London in 1779, p. 127

Indeed, during their stay in America, both Richard and William Howe had attempted unofficially to mediate a peaceful end to the rebellion, both were sympathetic to the American cause, and both hoped to redress what they viewed as just colonial grievances. For their pains, the Howe brothers found themselves embroiled for many years in a bitter controversy in Great Britain. Neither ever returned to America.

General Howe's deputy, Sir Henry Clinton, assumed supreme command of Britain's army in America. Sir Henry was well acquainted with the Province of New York. His father, Admiral George Clinton, had served there as royal governor during King George's War and young Henry had joined the New York militia upon coming of age. Henry Clinton earned his spurs during the Seven Years War in north Germany in 1759 as an infantry commander pitted against the French.[2] It is reasonable to suppose that memory of his early service in New York may have left an indelible mark on Sir Henry and, coupled with the city's obvious political and strategic value, may have colored his judgment concerning the American colonists and their uprising.

Upon the outbreak of hostilities in Boston in 1775, Sir Henry had been sent to America. He remained in His Majesty's service in America during the entire seven-year course of the American Revolution, being replaced by Sir Guy Carleton in February 1782. Clinton had served under Generals Gage and Howe, and indeed had devised the tactical plan that enabled General Howe to seize Long Island in September 1776. For this valuable assistance to the Crown, Clinton was knighted.

History paints a picture of General Sir Henry Clinton as highly intelligent and diligent, but also as risk averse to the point of indecision, critical and exacting of others, and coldly stubborn. He was not given to accepting with good grace either the advice

---

2 King George's War (1740-1748) was known in Europe as the War of the Austrian Succession. The Seven Years' War (1756-1763) was known in America as the French and Indian War (1754-1763).

or the criticism of others. Indeed, several times while serving under General Howe, Clinton had proffered tactical plans – some of which were quite sound – only to have Howe reject them out of hand. This caused a testy General Clinton to return to Great Britain at the end of 1776 for two months' leave with the intention of resigning. Only the granting of knighthood and persuasion by his (few) friends caused him to return to America in early 1777 to continue as deputy to Howe until the latter's resignation in May 1778.[3]

The situation in which Clinton found himself upon assuming supreme command in mid-year 1778 was not promising. The French had openly joined the war just as he assumed command, thus making Great Britain's military position far more complex. French naval power transformed what had been a localized conflict between the Mother Country and its disgruntled American subjects into merely one part of a now global war – pitting the French and British against one another in Europe, India, North America, the West Indies, and on the high seas. The addition of Spain to the list of Britain's enemies in 1779 and Holland in the following year did not make matters any better strategically for the British.

Sir Henry evidently did not comprehend that by 1778 military force alone was no longer sufficient to suppress the American rebellion. In contrast to Howe's approach of seizing territory – pushing back Washington's army and ultimately capturing the American "capital" at Philadelphia – and then holding out an olive branch, Sir Henry Clinton believed it necessary to trap Washington and destroy his army. Howe may have chosen his more deliberate strategy not only to conserve his own troop strength, but also

---

[3] Clinton's appointment as supreme commander was by no means popular in London. Rather, he was seen as the only available choice, and was reluctantly appointed after several more desirable officers refused to serve in America. See Hibbert, <u>Redcoats and Rebels</u>, pp. 201-211. Clinton had little political backing at home, had few friends, and was unpopular with his troops.

to signal to those colonists whose support for independence was wavering that victory inevitably lay with His Majesty's forces and that political reconciliation was possible. Indeed, as noted, William Howe had the somewhat contradictory mission of making war while holding out the prospect of an honorable peace.

Clinton probably did not consider the colonial rebellion to be subject to negotiation leading to a political settlement. His view almost certainly was that military force was to be used to stamp out the embers of rebellion. His Majesty's courts and gaols would punish the traitorous ringleaders for causing the war. There would be no need for British Peace Commissioners to treat with the American rebels as if they were equals.[4]

It is just possible, however, that given the drastically altered strategic situation in 1778, with French naval power suddenly thrown into the balance the policy community in London now considered that a negotiated peace with the Americans was imperative – albeit with certain limitations. Toward this end, in 1778 the British put out peace-feelers to see if the Americans would settle for internal autonomy under the Crown rather than outright independence. Perhaps British thinking was to entice the Americans to drop their French allies, thus freeing up British land and naval forces to concentrate solely on beating the French. Whatever thinking lay behind British political moves and peace offers in 1778, these thoughts and offers came to nothing.

---

4 Sir Henry Clinton wrote to Lord Cornwallis on 2 March 1781: "...*there seems little wanting to give a mortal stab to rebellion, but a proper reinforcement and a permanent superiority at sea...*" (London: J. Debret, 1783; [p.58.] Number II) in http://home.golden.net/marg/bansite/src/cornwallis0.html, hereafter referred to as Debret. Found at the website "Oatmeal for Foxhounds." Sir Henry's amazing statement indicates that he believed total victory possible over the Revolution even at this late date and displays his ignorance of the true situation in the American South. Cornwallis had not yet met Greene at Guilford Court House, but the "victory" at Guilford ended the British attempt to conquer the South.

The Carlisle Peace Commission, sent out in the late spring of 1778, offered what today would be called "Commonwealth" status to the Americans. But this offer was "too little, too late." Although Parliament repealed the most objectionable legislation that had galvanized the Americans to take up arms three years earlier, the Americans were past the stage of pleading for "the rights of Englishmen" and would settle for nothing less than complete independence of Great Britain. In November, the Earl of Carlisle and his associates returned to London empty-handed.

The British high command in America could show very little for three years of effort. Clinton had been ordered to abandon Philadelphia in 1778 – and the city promptly reverted to rebel control.[5] He did hold New York City in strength, but had only toeholds in Newport, Rhode Island, and the lower Hudson Valley outside the city. The rest of New York and New England was under rebel control. True, the British had near total command of the sea through Royal Navy squadrons on the American station. But Sir Henry's personal relationships with the admirals were touchy at best…and often quite bad. The British held a handful of bases along the Atlantic coast, but inland from the Atlantic – and away from the watchful protection of the Royal Navy – there were few secure British outposts. For all intents and purposes, with the exception of New York City and a few other places, the new "united States" had won its independence. Royal administrative control vanished almost as soon as His Majesty's armed forces departed from any given district.

It may have occurred to the British policy community as early as 1778 that the American war was essentially lost – at least in New England and the Middle Atlantic colonies. The failure of

---

[5] Without notifying the Carlisle Delegation, Lord Germain had directed Sir Henry Clinton to send 8,000 of his 14,000 men from Philadelphia to the West Indies. This rendered Philadelphia vulnerable to attack and thus obliged General Clinton and the Carlisle Delegation to withdraw to New York. (Tuchman, p. 223.)

the Carlisle mission showed that there was considerable distance between what Lord North's Ministry was prepared to offer and what the Continental Congress demanded. The best that could be hoped for, especially if British military resources were to be redirected against France before it was too late, was to salvage whatever could be saved from the wreckage of Britain's American empire.

This consideration may have caused British strategic thinking to focus upon the southern colonies of Georgia and the Carolinas. General Sir Henry Clinton, though maintaining his supreme headquarters in New York City, turned his gaze southward. With the return of the failed Carlisle mission to London in November 1778, British politico-military strategy shifted toward the reestablishment of British power in the American South.

The southern colonies, including the Province of Virginia, were considered to be of greater importance to British commerce and industry than were those of the Middle Atlantic or New England. The agricultural nature of the South fit in very well with the British Empire's mercantile system. British merchants obtained tobacco, indigo, rice, cotton, and other agricultural products from the American South. Moreover, the trade balance in favor of London merchants and their American-based "factors" was highly favorable. Not least, the British believed – with some justification – that there was substantial royalist sympathy to be found in the South. Perhaps, just perhaps, the colonists in the American South would rally to the Union Jack out of loyalty to His Majesty and from consideration of their trade relationships with the Mother Country.

London considered the views of the royal governors of the southern colonies who easily convinced Lord North and his Cabinet that many Loyalists would rise up to join the Crown.[6] Along with this political support, London could count on a continued flow of foodstuffs to the British West Indies – vital to feed the planters

---

6 Fortescue, pages 21 and 102-103.

and the populace there since little food was grown on the islands. Moreover, rebel income from the sale of indigo and tobacco that was used to pay for arms and ammunition could be cut off.

From the British perspective, if granting limited autonomy was insufficient to entice the Americans to the negotiating table, perhaps the four southern colonies could be forcibly detached from the other nine and a compromise peace arranged. The British then would cut their losses by granting "independence" to the northern colonies – which were, in any case, already lost – while retaining Virginia, the Carolinas, and Georgia as royal colonies under King George III. Despite their nominal independence, the nine northern colonies would be completely surrounded by British possessions[7] and would therefore remain dependent economically on the Empire. Their independence would mean little.

There was one strategic problem, however. Given the global French naval challenge to Great Britain – even in the English Channel itself – British naval and military strength in America was sufficient to maintain securely one major center of political power in the rebellious colonies. *But not two. And certainly not three or more.* Further complicating British planning was the sudden need to protect the British West Indies from possible French conquest. The Royal Navy's resources would be stretched to the limit.

If British land forces were deployed *en masse* in the Hudson Valley area, and protected by the Royal Navy from French interference, the Americans would be hard pressed to drive the British out and capture New York. Conversely, if all British land forces were committed wholeheartedly to the invasion and occupation of the American South – again making good use of naval support – it would be unlikely that the Americans, even with French land

---

7 George Rogers Clark did not capture Vincennes from the British until February 1779. If peace had been declared in 1778, the Ohio Valley would have remained in British hands thus effectively limiting the United Colonies to a western boundary resting on the Monongahela and Allegheny rivers.

armies and naval forces assisting, could dislodge them. Fortescue states that in 1775 senior British officers calculated that it would take between 30,000 and 50,000 British troops to occupy the line of the Hudson Valley, thereby isolating New England from the southern colonies and cutting off food supplies and military assistance.[8]

By maintaining two major centers of land power – supreme headquarters in New York City and another major force somewhere in the South – one or the other could be vulnerable to rebel attack. The Royal Navy could protect either British New York or the land force in the South, but it would be hard-pressed to protect both equally well while simultaneously challenging French naval power in the West Indies or in European waters. Both the Royal Navy and His Majesty's land forces in the American colonies would be divided into two merely strong, but not unassailable, forces. *What if the French and American land forces were able to concentrate against whichever of the two British centers of influence was the "more vulnerable?"*

From the British standpoint, the dilemma was simply this: *If we evacuate New York, as we did Philadelphia, what do we gain from this? Nothing. But if we concentrate all our forces in the southern colonies, can we be absolutely assured of victory? Perhaps this is possible if enough loyalists rally to the Crown. Can we retain New York City while at the same time dispatching a strong enough force to oust the rebels in the South and restore royal power from Savannah to Richmond? The outcome of this gamble depends upon the ability of the Americans and French to work together smoothly and efficiently. As events have shown, this has not always been the case.*

---

8 Fortescue, p. 19. With the entry of France into the war, the British did not have the 50,000 soldiers needed. Moreover, the logistical challenge of supporting such a massive force across 3,000 miles of ocean would have been insuperable. The resulting cost of such an expedition can be imagined.

Logistics was yet another complicating factor for the British. Armies must be regularly fed and clothed, and must have arms and ammunition and a variety of other supplies. Only sporadically – and often at exorbitant cost – could the British obtain provisions in the colonies. Many farmers either could not, or would not, sell their grain, beef, or dairy products to His Majesty's army commissary officers in America. Thus, the British army was compelled to set up an extensive re-supply network based on commercial sources in the British Isles to funnel vast quantities of foodstuffs and other needed supplies to a Royal Navy base at Cork, Ireland. From Cork food and other materials were transported across the Atlantic to the ports of New York (1776-1783) and Philadelphia (1777-1778) in the north and to Charleston in the south (after May 1780). Once in America supplies would be carried in wagons over the muddy roads to His Majesty's regiments.

A Member of Parliament is alleged to have quipped that British soldiers in America were *"fed from Leadenhall"* – a large covered market in London located in Gracechurch Street. General Howe's commissary agent recognized that provisions and supplies in the required quantities were not to be had in America: *"There is no dependence for supplies for the Army from this Continent."*[9] Indeed, the New England colonies had short growing seasons and generally poor soils. Even had the colonists living there enthusiastically supported the Crown – and they did not – there would have been little surplus to feed His Britannic Majesty's troops. The Middle Atlantic colonies had milder climates and better soils, but even in this region pickings were often slim. Washington and the American commissary agents could attest to that fact. New Jersey, for example, had been picked clean by both armies.

Perhaps the southern colonies, with their fertile soils and long growing seasons, might be better suited to offering meat

---

9 AmericanRevolution.org; "Chapter IV, The Organization of the British Army in the American Revolution, The Provisioning of the Army."

and produce to the British army. There were only two problems with this hypothesis. First, the colonial population in the South was dispersed over a wide area – much of the South was still a virtual wilderness, especially in the Piedmont. Second, the British presumed that the populace was more favorably disposed toward the Crown than proved to be the case.

Frankly, the policy decision to embark upon a southern campaign toward the end of 1778 was a gamble. But enough men of influence in London, such as Lord George Germain, the Secretary of State for the American Department, thought the risk was worth taking.

# V

# GLORY AND DANGER ALIKE

Some historians hold the view that, had the Carlisle Peace Commission[1] put its terms on the negotiating table in 1775, or even as late as Spring 1776, civil war in the British Empire could have been avoided. Had Great Britain granted its restive American colonies internal self-government under a kind of "commonwealth" arrangement as Thomas Pownall and others advocated, it is possible that the United Colonies of America would have remained tied to the Crown in much the same way as Canada and Australia are today.[2] That this did not happen was due largely to British political myopia, Parliamentary arrogance, and royal pigheadedness.

---

1  The peace delegation consisted of Frederick Howard, 5th Earl of Carlisle, Governor George Johnstone, and William Eden. Eden was manager of secret intelligence during the war and a friend of North, Germain, and Wedderburn. Johnstone, who had been governor of West Florida from 1763 to 1767, had attempted to bribe Robert Morris and Joseph Reed, was exposed and, humiliated, forced to resign. (Tuchman, p. 222)

2  Thomas Pownall had been governor of four different provinces, including Massachusetts, and was later elected to Parliament. Sympathetic to America, he stated in 1770: *"You may exert power over, but you can*

The Carlisle group arrived only in 1778. By the time that it opened correspondence with the Continental Congress then meeting in York, Pennsylvania, the "united States of America" had declared itself independent of the Crown, organized a shadow government (of sorts) and raised armed forces (again, of sorts.) It had been recognized as a separate country by a major European power, France. It had also won a resounding victory at Saratoga over a major British force and liberated a great part of its territory from colonial rule. The weak "united States" had not been overthrown by the loss of its "capital" Philadelphia in 1777, and the American army under Washington had survived a terrible winter of suffering at Valley Forge. Against all odds and expectations, Washington's army lived to fight on. Indeed, trained by Baron von Steuben and equipped by the French, the Continental Army showed remarkable resilience and in 1778 generally performed well.

> Without arrogance or the smallest deviation from truth it may be said that no history now extant can furnish an instance of an army's suffering such uncommon hardships as ours has done, and bearing them with the same patience and fortitude. To see men, without clothes to cover their nakedness, without blankets to lie on, without shoes, by which their marches might be traced by blood from their feet, and almost as often without provisions as with them, marching through the frost and snow, and at Christmas taking up their winter-quarters within a day's march of the enemy, without a house or hut to cover them, till they could be built, and submitting to it without a murmur, is a proof of patience and obedience, which in my opinion can scarce be paralleled.[3]

---

*never govern an unwilling people."* (Tuchman, p. 183) Edmund Burke said much the same.

3 George Washington's letter to John Bannister, 21 April 1778, after the terrible ordeal of Valley Forge. WGW: Fk, Vol. 11, pages 284-93.

By the end of 1778, the British thus found themselves in a trap of their own making. The French were anxious to redress the gross imbalance of power that had resulted from the catastrophe of the Seven Years War. They intended to secure for themselves valuable political and economic advantages in Europe and America and, into the bargain, they hoped to humble "perfidious Albion." British troop strength in America had ratcheted up to nearly 30,000 by April 1778,[4] yet the rebellious colonies seemed even further from submitting to the Crown than they had been just two years earlier. Adding to London's jitters was the possibility that Spain might join in the fray to retake Gibraltar, East and West Florida, and other Spanish possessions lost to Britain.

There could be little doubt that, were the British faced by only one opponent – whether the American rebels, the French, or the Spanish – they could bring to bear sufficient resources to deal with that particular opponent. However, London simply did not have the resources needed to handle all its enemies simultaneously. The strategic balance had shifted in 1778 and the London policy community knew it.

> But Lord Sandwich, the shrewd and hard-working (though personally notorious) First Lord of the Admiralty, recognized that the English navy was not strong enough to operate in European and American waters at the same time. Lord North, not Lord Sandwich, must bear the onus for reducing England's naval strength in 1772, an economy measure that had fatal consequences.[5]

---

4 "The British Army in America 1776 to 1781," http://www.redcoat.me.uk/armylists.htm

5 Richard Hofstadter, et al., p. 104. The Earl of Sandwich was acutely aware of his lack of naval resources due, ironically, to Lord North's cutback of the naval budget in 1772. North served as Chancellor of the Exchequer from December 1767 and retained that post after becoming Prime Minister in March 1770. He resigned both posts in March 1782 upon losing a vote of "No Confidence."

British strategic thinking probably shifted as well. From the single-minded concept of stamping out rebellion and re-imposing unquestioned royal authority in colonies, the London policy community now was confronted with the need to defend what it could and minimize British losses to the extent possible. This was especially true of the British West Indies and British possessions in India. America had thus become a kind of sticky political flypaper that tied down British armies, fleets, commanders, military supplies, and royal gold that were desperately needed elsewhere.

That the policy community in London took very seriously the change in the strategic situation in early 1778 is made clear by a comparison of national capabilities between Great Britain and France. All British policymakers, cabinet ministers, and Members of Parliament would have been aware of the basic facts of European power.

At the beginning of the American war in 1775 Great Britain with its population of about nine million faced only their thirteen rebellious American colonies which between them had perhaps barely three million inhabitants. (And even these three millions were by no means united in their quest for independence.) Moreover, compared to her colonies, Britain had overwhelming superiority in agricultural output, production of iron and general industrial production. The Bank of England, founded in 1694, was capable of marshalling great sums for the Crown's use. As is known, the treasury of the Continental Congress was empty and its credit highly questionable. Historians generally agree that the Industrial Revolution began in Great Britain in 1760 whereas America entered the Industrial Age only in 1820. The Royal Navy also had 73 ships-of-the-line whereas the Thirteen Colonies obviously had none at all.

But the Treaty of Alliance signed on 6 February 1778 between France and the thirteen rebellious colonies radically changed the strategic picture. With nearly 26 million inhabitants, France had a population three times that of Great Britain. Moreover, its iron output was twice that of Britain, and France greatly exceeded Great

Britain in both agricultural and industrial output. Only in ships-of-the-line did France lag Britain at the beginning of the war with 60. However, given the productivity of her shipyards, by 1780 France had built an additional 19 capital ships bringing her total to 79.

Even these statistics do not tell the full story of the power shift of 1778. France was regarded as the premier land power in Europe and her armies were considered both more numerous and better trained and equipped than any of her rivals. Moreover, French finances gave her "deep pockets" for waging war. She could also turn to her allies in Europe, such as Prussia and Poland, to obtain any military talent that might be needed.[6] Not least, French diplomats had considerable influence throughout Europe.

Equally sobering to the British political elite was the stark fact that Great Britain did not have a single ally. She now found herself entirely alone, mired in a global war that had grown from her mishandling of relatively minor colonial issues.

Spain added to British worries. Although Spain was a declining power by the 1770s, she nevertheless possessed a fleet of 49 ships-of-the-line and an enormous empire in the Americas. Spanish economic resources and military power would complicate British operations in the Mediterranean and the West Indies. If her fleet were added to that of the French, the advantage at sea would tilt heavily against the Royal Navy.

Holland might also be factored into the strategic balance. The British were well aware that the Dutch island of St. Eustatius was a key transit point for European war materials and other goods being smuggled to the Thirteen Colonies – some of which originated in Great Britain itself! The Dutch also were quite capable of making loans to the rebels and, with their extensive merchant fleet, of sustaining the flow of supplies across the Atlantic.

---

6 A case in point is the recruitment by the Comte de Vergennes of Friedrich Wilhelm von Steuben from Prussia who proved to be of inestimable value to George Washington in training Continental soldiers.

The shifting military balance on the European continent was not London's only worry. The British also found themselves facing the League of Armed Neutrality that effectively locked up the Baltic Sea trade – including vital naval stores and other supplies. Russian Empress Catherine the Great formed the League early in 1780 with Sweden and Denmark (which at the time ruled Norway). Although the League did not pose a military threat to Britain as did France and her ally, Spain, the League nonetheless hampered Great Britain economically by cutting off her access to vital sources of raw materials.

The gloomy strategic picture facing the London policy community presented only two possible courses of action – seek a negotiated peace immediately – or stake everything on one last throw of the dice. Although fully recognizing the danger, Lord North and his Secretary for American affairs, Lord George Germain, chose to gamble.

# VI

# Flying on "Canvas Wings"

Despite squeaks of protest from the Carlisle peace negotiators, Sir Henry Clinton stuck to his orders from Lord George Germain and, with suitable fanfare and colors flying, marched out of Philadelphia in June 1778.[1] British rule would never return to the "City of Brotherly Love" and the city would remain unmolested for the rest of the war. Clinton struck out across New Jersey for New York.

As General Clinton neared Monmouth, New Jersey, Washington attacked him in force. A furious battle ensued in which losses on both sides were about equal. Charles Lee's bizarre action in suddenly and inexplicably retreating from the field nearly cost

---

1 Mahan, <u>Influence of Seapower on History</u>, p. 162. London recognized the strategic danger to its land forces in Philadelphia given the French naval threat. Had Admiral d'Estaing arrived in Delaware Bay prior to the British evacuation, and Washington been able to position the Continental Army opposite Philadelphia, the British might have been decisively beaten. The Royal Navy would have been trapped in Delaware Bay (leaving New York unprotected) and the British land forces in both Philadelphia and New York vulnerable to siege.

Washington the battle, but Washington's conspicuous gallantry rallied his soldiers and the Continentals repelled every British counterattack.[2] Under cover of darkness, Sir Henry withdrew from the field and hastily made his way to the defenses of New York. Although tactically a draw, the Battle of Monmouth was a strategic victory for the Americans. British power in the Middle Atlantic was forever eliminated from New Jersey and confined to the lower Hudson for the remainder of the war.

As the Carlisle mission continued its feckless talks through the hot summer months, Sir Henry regrouped his forces and bided his time in New York. Washington hovered above him at White Plains in position to block or delay any British movement to the north. Matters appeared to have reached something of a stalemate by early 1779.

At the end of November the Earl of Carlisle and his party boarded ship for England. In many ways the Carlisle mission marked the watershed of the American war. From 1775 to 1778, the center of action was in the Middle Atlantic and New England theaters of war. After the brief "pause" in hostilities during the Carlisle talks of summer 1778, the last three years of the war would be fought in a different theater – the American South.

The day after Christmas 1778, again complying with orders from Germain, Sir Henry Clinton boarded ship with 3,500 British regulars bound for Savannah. Taking the city by surprise, the British under Lieutenant Colonel Archibald Campbell overwhelmed its militia defenders. The British had secured a foothold in the Province of Georgia. As George Washington had noted, the British army had made good use of its mobility thanks to the "canvas wings" of the Royal Navy. Command of the sea enabled the British to move swiftly to any point they wished along the coast. By contrast,

---

2 Charles Lee was subsequently court-martialed and drummed out of the army. WGW: Fk, Vol. 13, p. 448

American forces could move only as fast as the infantry could march overland. And colonial roads were poor.

Aiding Clinton's amphibious assault into the South was a column of British troops under General Augustine Prevost that marched north from British-held Florida into Georgia. Colonel Campbell proceeded up the Savannah River to seize Augusta in January 1779. The southern campaign, which was to prove decisive, had begun.

Ever the astute observer, Washington commented: *"the operations in the Southern States do not resemble a transient incursion, but a serious conquest."*[3]

The British strategic offensive in 1779 aimed at consolidating royal power in Georgia with the intention of crossing from Georgia into South Carolina. At the time, Georgia consisted of a thin line of counties bordering the Savannah River and westward from the river only some thirty or forty miles at most. Beyond this settled area, basically from the Ogeechee River westward, was Indian Territory that would remain a thorn in the side of the American settlers for another 50 years.

In the first half of 1779, General Prevost conducted a series of limited attacks designed to probe American strength in and around the key seaport of Charleston. Benjamin Lincoln was sent south with Continental troops to prevent Prevost from penetrating into South Carolina. American tactical successes, such as Andrew Pickens' victory at Kettle Creek in February, were offset by American failures, such as that at Briar Creek in March. Tactically, from March to late October 1779 there was a stalemate along the Savannah River. Prevost's greatest success, however, was in raising Tory confidence in Georgia and the Carolinas that a British victory was possible, even likely.

As summer gave way to fall, General Lincoln attempted to reduce Savannah by siege with the help of a French fleet and 4,000 soldiers under Admiral Comte d'Estaing. A deserter betrayed the assault

---

3 Ellis, p. 124.

to Prevost resulting in a Franco-American defeat with heavy loss. Polish Count Casimir Pulaski was killed in October. The failure of the siege and the changing winds of late October caused d'Estaing to weigh anchor, thus leaving General Lincoln with no option but to fall back on Charleston. This defeat caused the Americans to have bitter feelings toward the French while producing jubilation among the Tories. Sir Henry Clinton used this bitterness to advantage in his propaganda intended to sow discontent among the American troops in hopes of disrupting the Franco-American alliance. The successful defense of Savannah further encouraged the Tories to openly declare themselves for the Crown.

A private letter from Savannah, Georgia, printed in James Rivington's[4] *Royal Gazette* on 20 November 1779 had this to say about the denouement of the siege:

> The exact loss of the enemy [ie. the Patriot and French forces] cannot be ascertained; but Mr. Robert Baillie, who was a prisoner with the French during the whole siege, says they own a loss of near fifteen hundred. The count, in the action of the ninth, was wounded in the arm and thigh, and Pulaski very dangerously by a grape shot in the groin. Two days ago the last of the French troops embarked; the rebels have been gone some time, and we are now in as much tranquility as we have been for any time these six months past. *Mutual animosity and reviling have arisen to such a height between the French and rebels since they were defeated, that they were almost ready to cut one another's throats.*[5]

---

4 Research in 1959 discovered the fact that James Rivington, long believed to have been a violent Tory and editor of the British army's propaganda newspaper, *Royal Gazette*, was in fact one of Washington's spies. See Bakeless, p. 228. As Clinton's publicist, Rivington would have had unique access to Sir Henry, and would therefore have been in position to gauge Sir Henry's fears of attack – and perhaps even reinforce those fears.

5 Quoted in Frank Moore, Diary of the Revolution, p. 400. The count referred to is probably d'Estaing. Italics added for emphasis of the mutual

The British and Tories rejoiced over their victory and gloated about the falling out between the American rebels and their French allies. More significantly, the initiative now passed to the British. It would not be long before the British renewed their attempt to take Charleston and expand their operations into the Carolinas.

Despite royalist euphoria over d'Estaing's withdrawal and the rebel defeat, some more thoughtful British senior officers drew a deeper lesson from the event. They recognized how vulnerable His Majesty's land armies would be if the French were to gain even local superiority at sea. Many months later, Sir Henry Clinton wrote to his superior in London, Lord George Germain, the following illuminating letter about sea power:

> For, with regard to our efforts in the Chesapeak, your Lordship knows how much their success and even the safety of the armament there will depend upon our having a decided naval superiority in these seas. And I, therefore, cannot doubt that every precaution will be taken, to give me, at least, timely notice of the contrary being likely to happen; as my ignorance of such an event might be most fatal in its consequences.[6]

The Americans and French also learned a few things from the Savannah debacle. Chief among these was that the closest possible cooperation and coordination between land and naval forces was required if they were to achieve victory. In their written instructions to Rochambeau in 1780 the French showed that this lesson had been learned.

---

recriminations occurring between French and Americans following the failed siege. As noted, Rivington published pro-British news stories given him by Sir Henry Clinton.

6 Letter, Sir Henry Clinton to Lord George Germain, 5 April 1781. See "Oatmeal for Foxhounds" at http://home.golden.net/-marg/bansite/src/clintonnarrative.html.

Superior British mobility, made possible yet again by their "canvas wings," permitted Sir Henry to remove his garrison from Newport, Rhode Island, and deploy the troops for the long-planned siege of Charleston, South Carolina. In late December 1779 Clinton sailed with 8,000 regulars to attack Charleston in concert with Prevost and local Tory forces. Sir Henry's arrival brought the total number of British Empire forces to about 14,000 to oppose Lincoln's army of 5,400 men.

The siege of Charleston began in earnest in February. Admiral Marriot Arbuthnot's fleet bottled up the harbor and began shelling Charleston while Sir Henry completed his siege works around the city by 11 April. Given overwhelming odds in his favor, and Clinton's ability to bombard Charleston at will from every direction, British victory over the Americans was inevitable.

Benjamin Lincoln surrendered on Friday, 12 May 1780, the worst drubbing suffered by the American side during the war. The terms of surrender were typical of the time, with the exception that the "honors of war" usually accorded to a defeated foe were denied:

> May 12. – Yesterday the British advanced within thirty yards of the American lines, and commenced preparations for a combined assault by sea and land. The reduced state of the garrison, the urgent solicitations of the inhabitants, and the clamors of the soldiery, compelled General Lincoln to renew negotiations with the British commanders; and to-day the articles of capitulation have been signed. It is stipulated that the Continental troops and sailors shall remain prisoners of war until exchanged, and be supplied with good and wholesome provisions, in such quantity as is served out to the British troops. The militia are to return home as prisoners on parole, which, as long as they observe, is to secure them from being molested in their property by British troops. The officers of the army and navy are to keep their swords, pistols, and baggage, which is not to be searched, and are to retain their servants. The garrison, at an appointed hour, is to march out of town, to the ground between the works and the canal, where they are to deposit their arms. The drums are not to beat a British march, nor the colors to be uncased. All civil

officers and citizens who have borne arms during the siege, are to be prisoners on parole, and with respect to their property within the city, they are to have the same terms as the militia. All persons in the town, not described in any article, are, notwithstanding, to be prisoners on parole. It is left to future discussion whether or no a year shall be allowed to all such as do not choose to continue under the British government, to dispose of their effects real and personal, in the state, without any molestation whatever, or to remove such part thereof as they choose, as well as themselves and families, and whether, during that time, they, or any of them, shall have it in their option to reside occasionally in town or country. The French consul, the subjects of France and Spain, with their houses, papers, and other movable property, are to be protected and untouched; but they are to consider themselves as prisoners on parole.[7]

Sir Henry, more than satisfied with his victory in Charleston, now availed himself of his "canvas wings" to return to New York with part of his forces while leaving his deputy, Lord Charles Cornwallis, with 8,000 soldiers to finish the job in the South.

History records a rocky relationship between Sir Henry Clinton and his subordinate, Lord Charles Cornwallis. In part, this tension was caused by their differing temperaments. As noted, Clinton was cerebral but not especially personable. He insisted on drafting meticulous plans for every contingency, and though he could be tactically imaginative on paper Sir Henry was anything but bold and decisive on the battlefield. We might judge that Clinton would have made a superlative staff officer, but as a commander of troops he was at best mediocre.

Cornwallis clearly was a "man of action." He wished to take the battle to the rebels and was ready at any moment to attack enemy forces when and wherever found. Cornwallis was a gifted battlefield commander and certainly was not lacking in personal courage. His

---

[7] Moore, pp. 416-7

principal shortcoming was perhaps a failure to understand the nature of the war in which he found himself and his ignorance of the strategy appropriate to such a war.

Both men were agreed on the following basic goals: rebel forces in the South must be destroyed, Tory Loyalists must be encouraged to declare for the Crown, and the southern colonies must be pacified. However, Cornwallis and Clinton were at some variance as to how to go about achieving those ends. Had he been in command of the British forces in the South, although speculative, it is possible that Sir Henry might have employed what might be called a "coastal approach" in conquering the Carolinas. Clinton's campaign would have moved methodically northward staying as close as possible to the coast to remain in contact with the Royal Navy, occupying ports and centers of population, and attempting some sort of "consolidation" as he advanced. But Clinton was hundreds of miles away to the north and, in any case, was consumed in defending New York from possible attack by Washington.

Cornwallis used what might be described as an "overland approach" that focused upon rallying Tories and destroying American forces. Where rebel commanders such as General Horatio Gates attempted to use conventional units conventionally, as at Camden, Cornwallis was assured of victory – even with numerically inferior numbers. But later, against the elusive and wily General Nathanael Greene who used an unconventional Fabian "cat and mouse" approach that made good use of time, distance, and difficult terrain, Cornwallis was stymied.

It is likely that neither Sir Henry Clinton nor Lord Charles Cornwallis comprehended the nature of the war, the expansive terrain of America, or the attitudes of the colonists. General Clinton had prescribed for Cornwallis a route of march northward along the Carolina coast that would have led through river deltas, swamps, and unproductive countryside. Sir Henry justified his cautious "coastal approach" in the belief that the Royal Navy could keep a watchful eye over His Majesty's land forces, re-supplying them regularly and, should the need arise, evacuate them with minimal loss. Despite his personal squabbles with naval commanders, Clinton evidently valued these "canvas wings" more highly than did Cornwallis.

Lord Cornwallis kept his own counsel. Rather than proceed along the South Carolina shore as Sir Henry recommended, he struck out boldly into the heart of the colony to seize towns and defeat rebel units. His reasoning was that the interior offered better opportunity for maneuver and open battle and, in any case, the ability to live off the land. Many of the more productive farms were located at places like Ninety Six which was well inland. Perhaps, had Cornwallis either had a secure line of communication to ensure timely receipt of supplies and reinforcements from Charleston, or the enthusiastic support of the Carolina colonists, his overland advance might have been appropriate. He had neither.

In part, Lord Cornwallis was a victim of his ignorance of the geography and political conditions in the interior of South Carolina. In part, as events would prove, he was also a victim of the high-handed actions of his superior, Sir Henry Clinton.

After the fall of Charleston in May 1780, there was little further organized resistance, as almost every Patriot in South Carolina had been captured or had surrendered and taken parole. Only small bands of guerrillas led by Sumter, Pickens, and Marion continued to resist the British in the swamps and backcountry.

The problem in South Carolina was that the rule of law in the backcountry had collapsed. In the years before the Revolution there were few courthouses or county officers in the backcountry. The planter aristocracy and merchants of the coastal cities were slow to extend governance into the backwoods. For this reason there was near total anarchy with bands of outlaws roaming the countryside pillaging and burning. Citizens did band together as "Regulators" to enforce frontier justice until after 1769 when courthouses were built and county officers appointed. Even then animosity lingered and feuds simmered.

When the British invasion of the South began in 1780, people took sides just as much to settle old scores as for political reasons.

Tories were treated harshly as traitors and their lands were confiscated. When Sir Henry Clinton conquered Charleston, he did not reestablish even such civil governance as had then existed. Tories denied legal redress therefore resorted to the gun, torch, and rope for justice. This was only made worse by Clinton's stupidity and total lack of appreciation of the rights of the people by issuing a proclamation requiring all colonists to take an oath of allegiance to the Crown and if so required, to serve in His Majesty's forces. This act violated the terms of the paroles that Sir Henry Clinton and Lord Cornwallis had made with all the surrendering South Carolina patriots. Many of these men therefore once again took up arms against the British.

South Carolina rapidly descended into a bloody, brutal and complicated civil war. Shortly after issuing his proclamation, Sir Henry Clinton boarded a ship and sailed back to New York City leaving Cornwallis holding the bag. Cornwallis had one brief window of opportunity after the Battle of Camden when again there was no organized resistance and even the partisans were disheartened. But the absence of governance and the collapse of civil order in the backcountry would prove fatal for Cornwallis' hope of restoring royal authority in the Carolinas.

As it happened, the deeper Cornwallis advanced into the Carolina Piedmont, the longer his line of communications to Charleston became. Partisan units, such as those under Francis Marion and Andrew Pickens, aided by a slowly growing number of anti-British colonists, threatened Cornwallis' ever-longer and increasingly vulnerable logistical system. The further Lord Cornwallis advanced the more vulnerable he became.

Moreover, Cornwallis was anything but conciliatory and forgiving to the rebellious colonists. His "stern measures" taken against Carolinians suspected of Patriot sympathies did little to win those colonists back to enthusiastic support of British rule. Indeed, his "stern measures" arguably created more rebels from many Carolinians who simply wished to be left in peace and who had supported neither side in the conflict.

British military strategy did achieve part of the policy objective set in London. The successful defense of Savannah and the subsequent capture of Charleston – at the time the wealthiest and most populous city in the South – did much to encourage Tory Loyalists to openly declare for the Crown. Hundreds of Tories joined units under leaders such as Patrick Ferguson. It should also be remembered that many thousands of colonists were opposed to the political break with the Crown and did form a potential base of support for the reestablishment of royal rule – had that base of support been amply supported by a political strategy that would have underpinned British military moves.

However, the lack of a political strategy for the restoration of British colonial rule in the South was perhaps more fatal to Cornwallis than was his decision to ignore Clinton's advice about staying close to the Atlantic. Instead of following a policy of reconciling those colonists having grievances against the Crown, winning the sympathy of "neutrals" and giving active support to Loyalists, Lord Cornwallis punished the rebels, antagonized the "neutrals" and kept the Loyalists in decidedly subordinate roles. He flatly refused to restore civil rule in South Carolina, preferring to serve as that colony's military governor. In effect, General Cornwallis declared South Carolina to be a conquered enemy state rather than liberated friendly royal territory under its own civil (albeit pro-British) authorities.

Given South Carolina's prewar condition of lawlessness, Cornwallis' use of his military forces and his lack of a viable political strategy resulted in widespread violence throughout the Carolina Piedmont. Tory Loyalists now fell upon their neighbors who were suspected of Patriot sympathies. For their part, colonists who held anti-British sympathies and desired independence clashed with their Tory neighbors. Very soon the Carolina backlands were plunged into chaos with one neighbor fighting another. Much of this rural bloodletting is only poorly documented, but it was nevertheless quite real.

Moreover, the absence of responsible civil authority capable of maintaining some semblance of order in South Carolina left the region ungovernable by either side and vulnerable to the spread of insurgent units that menaced the roads on which Cornwallis depended. This meant that in reality Cornwallis did not have a secure rear area. He was therefore unwittingly advancing steadily forward into a quagmire of his own making.

In the summer of 1780 Lord Cornwallis moved inland into South Carolina meeting with almost continual military successes. The unwise General Horatio Gates, victor of Saratoga, was humbled at Camden on 16 August when he attempted to oppose Cornwallis in conventional battle. Nine hundred American soldiers lay dead or wounded, and another one thousand were made prisoners as Gates himself fled ignominiously 160 miles to safety.[8] Cornwallis and his cavalry commander, Lieutenant Colonel Banastre Tarleton, destroyed smaller rebel forces at Waxhaws and Fishing Creek with great savagery. An observer reporting to his superiors in September 1780 probably would have concluded that the American Revolution – at least the rebellion in the South – had been decisively defeated.

But was it? It was certainly true that a good number of Tories did rally to His Majesty as Cornwallis's victories convinced them of the inevitability of a royal triumph. That was part of the plan outlined by the policy community in London. But at the same time the British army's viciousness and cruelty -- especially by Tarleton and the Tory forces -- enraged large numbers of colonists in the Carolinas. The British invasion merely polarized the political struggle in the southern colonies, with neighbors now killing their neighbors. British military operations did little to cement royal control in the South.

The Battle of Camden, though a disaster for the American side, had one positive aspect. Recognizing the gravity of the deteriorating

---

8 Gates had 3,700 men at Camden; Cornwallis fielded only 2,100. Johan de Kalb, a friend of Lafayette's who had come to America with the Marquis, was killed at Camden.

situation in the South, and the failure of the boastful Gates to stop the advancing British, Congress returned overall command to George Washington in early October. Washington lost no time in appointing his trusted aide, Nathanael Greene, to command American forces in the South.

It was also in September 1780, with the southern colonies now in clear danger of being overrun by Lord Cornwallis, that Washington and his French allies began formulating a strategic plan that was to lead to the decisive victory that would end the war. That strategic plan was to pin as many British soldiers as possible in the defenses of New York while carefully laying the groundwork required to eventually trap or destroy a steadily weakening British expeditionary force somewhere in the South the moment it became vulnerable to allied land and sea power.

Now far from his base at Charleston and well away from the Atlantic coast, Cornwallis suffered two sharp defeats – the first at King's Mountain in October 1780 and the second at Cowpens in January 1781. Although Cowpens is justly regarded as "The American Cannae" – a clever double envelopment of the British that destroyed Tarleton's forces – the Battle of King's Mountain better illustrates what was taking place in the Carolina backlands. This is because King's Mountain was fought between 1,100 Tories under Major Patrick Ferguson and about 1,400 Virginia and Carolina militia and Tennessee "Over-mountain men" (including many sharpshooters) under Colonels Shelby and Campbell. The only Englishman in the fight was Major Ferguson. Patriot forces surrounded and decimated the Tory forces. Some 300 Tory Loyalists were killed, some were shot while trying to surrender, and another 700 of the force were captured. After the battle, the victorious – and vindictive – Patriots held a drumhead court in which ten captured Tories were tried and hanged for allegedly pillaging Patriot homes.

> This disaster [ed. King's Mountain] combined with widespread disorders in South Carolina, led Cornwallis to abandon a planned invasion of North Carolina. He retreated to winter quarters at Winnsborough, N.C., and took stern measures against rebellious colonists.[9]

The British strategy in the South was coming unraveled. Although it had started off well with the seizure of Savannah and Charleston, and was given a great boost by Gates' defeat at Camden, it slipped the track as Cornwallis moved inland. As noted, Cornwallis' "stern measures" did not transform rebels into loyal subjects of the Crown, and his inept political moves denied him a secure rear area. Moreover, Lord Cornwallis realized that his army was now far from its coastal bases and the protection of the Royal Navy. Not least, the British army found itself deep in a countryside swarming with guerrillas, such as those led by Pickens and Marion, and surrounded by a populace that was at best coldly neutral and often actively hostile.

Ever the astute strategist, and constantly informed of political and military conditions far and near, George Washington undoubtedly was aware of Lord Cornwallis' growing difficulties – and his shrinking resources. His Majesty's army in the South had dropped from 8,000 at Charleston to perhaps 5,000 as it invaded South Carolina, then probably to about 3,000 as the need to leave garrisons in occupied Georgia and the Carolinas depleted manpower as the British invasion rolled northward. Moreover, sickness, desertion and death took their toll. Indeed, at Camden Cornwallis used only 2,100 soldiers to rout Gates' force of some 3,700. But units on the move require more supplies than do those in garrison, and their casualty rates also are significantly higher. Washington might have pondered just how long Cornwallis could maintain an effective force in the field, given a hostile countryside, difficult terrain, and unreliable logistics.

---

9 Dupuy, page 719 (see Comment)

# VII

## ALLIES AND TRAITORS

The fall of Charleston in May 1780 and British triumphs in the South set in motion a series of events that led to a change in the strategic situation in America, and perhaps hastened Benedict Arnold's decision to defect to the British. The American disaster at Camden on 16 August 1780 clearly pointed to a growing and very serious British threat not merely to the southern colonies but to the American Revolution as a whole.

By placing the Southern Department under the independent command of the impetuous General Horatio Gates, Congress had effectively sidetracked Washington. For much of the summer of 1780 Washington could do little more than focus his attention on British New York and the immediately surrounding areas as the military situation in the South deteriorated. Indeed, from August to October 1780 it appeared that Lord Cornwallis had a virtually free hand in the Carolinas and could do as he pleased.

While the South was falling under British control, Benedict Arnold was in secret correspondence with Sir Henry Clinton via Major John Andre. This correspondence had begun as early as 1778 and was already well advanced by July 1780. From the spring of 1780, and perhaps at British instigation, Arnold pestered

Washington continually, insisting he be appointed commandant of West Point. Arnold even rejected offers of several prestigious field commands since it was his secret intention of turning over the fortress to Clinton and thereby opening the Hudson Valley to the British. Washington reluctantly granted Arnold's request in August.

The French under the Comte de Rochambeau and Admiral de Ternay landed at Newport, Rhode Island three months after Sir Henry had removed his garrison to begin his campaign in the South. However, with New England by now essentially liberated from British rule, a French garrison at Newport would be of little value strategically. Commencement of a siege of New York City might be a better use of the French land and naval power now based in Rhode Island.

Rochambeau landed 6,000 men at Newport on 10 July 1780, but he would not throw his army against the British without the protection of a fleet, reinforcements, and a clear plan of attack. In the summer of 1780, the French fleet was in the West Indies, the additional troops were in France, and the "clear plan of attack" did not exist.

Washington proposed to the French a meeting at Hartford, Connecticut, for 20 September 1780. He informed Arnold of the meeting on 14 September and requested a barge and guards to cross the Hudson. Washington asked Arnold to tell no one about his secret visit to the French. As Hughes notes laconically, *"Arnold did not tell anybody but Clinton."*[1]

After crossing the Hudson on Arnold's barge, Washington went on to Hartford where he made his first contact with his new French allies, Rochambeau and Admiral de Ternay.

Very little documentation survives from the September 1780 Hartford conference. What does survive is a joint request to Louis XVI for ships, men, and money signed by the three principals:

---

1 Hughes, p. 546

Washington, Rochambeau, and de Ternay. The Marquis de Lafayette, by now one of Washington's closest and most trusted aides, served as interpreter for the meeting. Although a larger group of French and American officers attended this first meeting, it appears that at some point Rochambeau, de Ternay, and Washington, with Lafayette acting as interpreter, closeted themselves for a private conversation. It is likely that during this private conversation, the French told Washington bluntly that their land and naval forces were insufficient for an attack on New York.

Only four days before the Hartford meeting opened, Lafayette had written to Chevalier de La Luzerne concerning the possibility of joint Franco-American operations in both the North and the South. The key to his letter – undoubtedly a key point discussed at length by Rochambeau, de Ternay, and Washington at Hartford – concerned the naval situation at New York.

> To the Chevalier de La Luzerne
> At headquarters, September 17, 1780
>
> For some time, Monsieur le Chevalier, we have been given over to all the vicissitudes of hope and fear. M. de Guichen's arrival is announced to us from so many sides that it is hard not to credit it. Yesterday we learned that Admiral Rodney had arrived off Sandy Hook with thirteen ships and that, joining Arbuthnot, he was going either to await M. de Guichen or to undertake an attack on Rhode Island in cooperation with General Clinton. After a restless night I was told this morning that the ships in question have entered within the Hook, and according to this news we have reason to hope that the supposed Rodney is only Admiral Arbuthnot hiding in New York Harbor. If this is so, we dare yet flatter ourselves that the great expedition is possible.
>
> We can have about twelve thousand Continentals; they say M. de Guichen has three thousand men; M. de Rochambeau, four. We shall muster ten thousand militia. As for provisions, we shall use force, and for such an occasion the people will not find it wrong. If it is possible for M. de Guichen to force New York Harbor, our expedition is certain; if he maintains naval

superiority outside the harbor, it is still possible. At least that is my private opinion; *but the harbor is the attractive point.*

*If our flag prevails here and if New York is not attacked, we absolutely must go to the South, and you will be very much of my opinion.* We are just leaving for Hartford, where we shall see the French generals. I wish you could be there, not only for the pleasure of seeing you, but for reasons of a public nature. I have not received any reply to what I had the honor to write to you on that subject. Colonel Tilghman, who is staying here, has taken charge of seeing that your letters reach me with all speed. I really wish these gentlemen might be informed of our situation by you. Although I am a little calmer since this morning, I am still very worried about this news of Rodney. If our squadrons make their junction, I shall at least be reassured about our chance of misfortune. M. de Guichen will be equal to the enemy, and, prejudice aside, I believe that from that time he would be superior, and all the more so since in case of emergency his retreat would be better executed.

If there is the least news on this subject, I have charged Colonel Tilghman to write you immediately. M. de Pontgibaud had only one packet for you, delivered by a merchant and entrusted to his care with little sense of urgency; he sent it by the post the day after he arrived, but I reprimanded him for it nonetheless. The ministers' letters were in M. de Vauban's hands, but Landais said he did not know those gentlemen.

Dare I ask you to tell M. de Loyaute that if I do not answer him immediately it is because I am trying to give a favorable response, of which I am very doubtful in view of our circumstances. M. de Galvan is in my light division and seems satisfied; I am infinitely so with him. Farewell, Monsieur le Chevalier; accept the assurance of my tender attachment.

Lafayette[2]

---

2 Letter of Marquis de Lafayette to Chevalier de La Luzerne, 17 September 1780. Italics added for emphasis. The discussion at Hartford turned on the naval situation. See Idzerda, Vol. III, p. 174.

What must be kept in mind is that by 1780 Washington had several highly effective spy networks in British occupied New York. These included not only the famous Culper Ring, but the Hendricks brothers, the Mersereau family, Hercules Mulligan and, among many other spies, none other than James Rivington, Sir Henry's publicist. Indeed, American spies had stolen the Royal Navy's codebooks in 1779 and presented them to the French.[3] Washington and the French were thus under no illusions whatsoever about British naval and military strength on York Island (Manhattan) and surrounding waters. Indeed, as mentioned by Lafayette, Admiral Sir George Rodney had arrived on 13 September 1780 with ten ships-of-the-line from the West Indies to reinforce Admiral Marriot Arbuthnot's squadron.

From the sketchy Minutes of Hartford, it appears that Washington and the French officers were completely agreed that *"there can be no decisive enterprise against the English naval establishments in this country without a constant naval superiority."*[4] Encouraged by the French presence at Newport – but perhaps overestimating their strength and capabilities – Washington took with him to the Hartford meeting an eight-page proposal for an assault on New York City. Through the Marquis de Lafayette, Washington proffered his plan with the hope that powerful Franco-American land and sea forces could attack New York before winter set in.

The French commanders, perhaps reflecting more soberly on their modest capabilities, and the risks of a premature assault on Sir Henry Clinton and the Royal Navy, set down their own thoughts. Rochambeau and Admiral de Ternay presented their proposals and assessments, along with their doubts and concerns. Almost certainly the French commanders highlighted hard tactical realities, which Lafayette translated into English for Washington. In his turn, Washington gave his responses translated into French

---

3 Bakeless, p. 228.

4 Idzerda, Vol. III, pp. 174-75.

for Rochambeau and de Ternay. In this manner a rough exchange of views began to shape what would become allied strategy for the final year of the war. What soon became abundantly clear to Washington was that, welcome as the French naval and land forces were, they were far from sufficient to dislodge Sir Henry Clinton from his comfortable headquarters on Manhattan.

From Washington's July 1788 letter to Noah Webster, it appears that the fundamental Franco-American strategy was laid down at Hartford in September 1780 for the final year of the war. And that strategy was laid down on the basis of cold, sober evaluation of British naval capabilities, the difficulty facing French vessels in passing the shallow waters of Sandy Hook, and the nature of Manhattan as something of a powerful fortress surrounded by a moat.

The Hartford conference ended on Friday, 22 September. The few notes taken indicate that the French were greatly impressed by the tall American general whose courtesy and quiet dignity somewhat overcame their doubts about the viability of the American cause that he served. Rochambeau and de Ternay returned to Newport on Friday. Saturday morning George Washington departed Hartford to return to his command just above New York in the town of Haverstraw.

Providentially, during his return to his headquarters at Haverstraw on Saturday, 23 September, Washington met the Chevalier de La Luzerne somewhere east of the Hudson. At the insistence of the gracious Chevalier Washington turned back, accompanying the Frenchman to Litchfield, Connecticut, where he stayed overnight. Ironically, Washington breakfasted Sunday morning the 24$^{th}$ in Fishkill, New York, with Joshua Hett Smith – a friend of none other than Major John Andre, adjutant general to Sir Henry Clinton.

As it happened, the very day that Washington was meeting with Rochambeau and de Ternay in Hartford, Thursday, 21 September, found John Andre and Benedict Arnold deep in conversation at Joshua Hett Smith's fine home on the west bank of the Hudson River. The two conspirators were discussing final plans for the surrender of West Point and Sir Henry Clinton's victory march up the Hudson. Andre had arrived in full uniform aboard the sloop *Vulture* which now lay at anchor in the river.

While Arnold and Andre talked and sipped tea at Joshua Smith's house, a "meddlesome (American) officer," one Colonel James Livingston, took it into his head to drive off the British ship.[5] Borrowing a small cannon and some powder, Livingston peppered the *Vulture* so vigorously that she retired down the river some distance. Livingston's trivial act completely overthrew Benedict Arnold's conspiracy.

While the *Vulture* was now safely out of range of Colonel Livingston's cannon, it was also out of range of the oarsmen who were to ferry Major Andre to the sloop and safety. In consternation, the two conspirators now made several operational blunders that were to prove fatal for Andre, though fortuitous for George Washington personally and for the American revolutionary cause. The Joshua Hett Smith house at Haverstraw[6] was Washington's headquarters, and nearby West Point was the key to the control of the Hudson River. Chance had foiled Arnold's carefully laid plans to betray West Point to Sir Henry Clinton and expose George Washington to almost certain capture.

Late on Friday the 22$^{nd}$, Major Andre – now dressed in civilian clothing – and Joshua Hett Smith set out by horse down the east bank of the Hudson, successfully clearing several checkpoints. However, despite General Arnold's pass made out in the name of "John Anderson," early the next morning three militiamen stopped Major Andre near Tarrytown. The militiamen frisked Andre and

---

5 Hughes, p. 549

6 The house was actually owned by Joshua's brother, Thomas Smith, but occupied by Joshua and his wife who had met John Andre, then a guest, there around 1775. Later called "Treason House," the dwelling was demolished. Joshua Hett Smith was tried for treason at Tappan but not convicted for lack of evidence.

discovered what appeared to be the plans of West Point tucked in Andre's boot. Andre was arrested as a spy.[7] Hearing of Andre's unexpected capture on Saturday morning by his own militiamen, Benedict Arnold lost no time saving his neck by escaping down the Hudson to the safety of the British defenses.

Washington was thunderstruck by Arnold's treachery. He understood at once the implications for West Point, his own person, and the fate of the Revolution. Moreover, Washington knew immediately that any and all operational plans to which Arnold might have had access were compromised to the British. The extent of the damage done probably took months to piece together (if indeed, it was ever fully pieced together).

Even without a fully researched damage assessment in hand, Washington understood that Sir Henry Clinton now had clear and precise knowledge of American strengths, dispositions, and – most importantly – plans. At least, General Clinton knew whatever Benedict Arnold knew as of Saturday, September 23rd.

Fortunately for the American cause, Benedict Arnold knew nothing of what had been discussed and agreed at Hartford with the French. He knew only that a meeting with Rochambeau and de Ternay had been held. But he knew nothing of its substance.

Perhaps the worst consequence of Arnold's treachery was its heavy psychological impact. With Arnold's defection to the British, a paralyzing black cloud of suspicion fell over the American command. In frustration and desperation, Washington is reported to have said: *"Whom can we trust now?"*[8]

Even so, despite his shock, rage and despair over the situation, Washington steadied himself and rallied his officers. Although American morale now appeared to be as low as at any time since

---

7 After trial by a board of officers, Andre was hanged on 2 October 1780 with Washington's reluctant approval.

8 Hughes, p. 553

the defeats of fall 1776, events in the South were to take a new and potentially decisive turn.

On 6 October 1780 Congress returned command in the South to Washington. With this renewed authority, Washington immediately appointed his trusted subordinate Nathanael Greene to command such American forces as remained in the Southern Department. As noted, one day later Patriot forces annihilated a large Tory force under Major Ferguson at King's Mountain in South Carolina. Guerrilla forces under Andrew Pickens and Francis Marion continued their attacks on isolated British units and outposts. All was not lost.

Perhaps there was one very positive outcome from Arnold's treachery. Ever the soul of discretion, Washington now more than ever realized that the fate of the Revolution depended upon the highest order of secrecy. Washington at once instituted what today would be called "compartmentation" and the "need to know" principle. Only those few, such as Rochambeau, de Ternay, Lafayette, and Washington himself, who had an absolute need to know what had been decided at Hartford, would share this secret knowledge.[9] All others, however loyal, would be told only as much as they needed to know in order to perform their duties. Nothing would be committed to paper.

---

9 Admiral de Ternay died in Connecticut on 15 December 1780 and was replaced first by Admiral Destouches and then, in May 1781, by the Comte de Barras. It is reasonable to believe that these two naval officers, as successors to de Ternay, were made aware of the allied grand strategy formulated at and after Hartford and the deception operation intended to mask allied moves and mislead the British.

# VIII

# POINT OF DECISION: NORTH OR SOUTH?

Since the days of Alexander the Great military commanders customarily have met with their principal subordinates to consider various alternative courses of action before setting in motion their combat forces and supply trains. A commander usually will seek the advice of his colleagues as to the feasibility of each possible course of action laid out by his staff. Today, Division and Corps G-3 (Operations) officers identify possible alternative courses of action. These staff officers consider the impact of terrain, weather, enemy capabilities, and other factors that either facilitate or hamper the accomplishment of the commander's mission. Some options will be dropped from consideration at an early stage for various reasons, usually because they are too costly or simply not feasible. However, when the Commanding General presides over a "council of war" he, along with his subordinate commanders, will study the remaining alternatives and choose the course they believe will best achieve the unit's objective with greatest speed, the least possible risk, and the lowest possible cost in lives and treasure.

In September 1780 George Washington had basically three alternative courses of action to choose from. He could concentrate his forces in the North where Sir Henry Clinton held New York City

# POINT OF DECISION: NORTH OR SOUTH?

with roughly 10,000 troops, artillery, and Royal Navy support.[1] Alternatively, Washington could seek a decisive engagement in the South where Lord Charles Cornwallis, constantly on the move through the Carolinas, had perhaps 3,000 to 5,000 men at that time.[2] His third alternative was, of course, to do nothing.

Doing nothing was exactly what Washington appeared to be doing – at least from the optic of the French Court and many in Congress. But despite his well-founded caution, never risking an open battle that would destroy his meager forces, Washington was not a man to sit around idly waiting for someone else to take the initiative. He was bent on some positive action. Yet he knew that his troop strength was not sufficient to permit him to meet on equal terms in open battle regular British forces anywhere in the colonies. So his decision boiled down to deciding where the application of his limited military power – north or south – would have the greatest chance of military success and, with that success, the greatest political impact both at home and in Great Britain.

New York appeared to be the obvious target. It was Sir Henry's supreme headquarters and he was Britain's supreme commander in America. The city was an important seaport and a center of population. New York also had symbolic value to both sides. Its capture by the Americans would deal a serious blow to the war party supporting Lord North's government. By the same token,

---

1 On 9 June 1781 Clinton reported to Germain that he had 9,997 soldiers. Two days later he wrote to Cornwallis that he had 10, 931 soldiers. Whatever the correct figure, this number was more than adequate to defend New York from any possible amphibious assault, given prepared positions and good intelligence.

2 Total British forces in the Carolinas and Georgia in the last six months of 1780 was probably about 10,000 of all kinds (British, Hessian, Tory) and yet, because of the need to place garrisons along the way, as Lord Cornwallis advanced, his maneuver force continually grew smaller. The arrival of General Leslie after the disaster at King's Mountain helped to temporarily boost Cornwallis' numbers. See "The British Army in America 1776 to 1781" at www.redcoat.me.uk/armylists.htm.

Patriots in New England and the Middle Atlantic colonies would hail its liberation and the surrender of Sir Henry Clinton.

Even before the French naval and land forces occupied Newport in July 1780, and certainly for many weeks thereafter, Washington maintained contact with Rochambeau and de Ternay through a series of letters often penned by Lafayette.[3] It is clear from the tenor of these letters that prior to his exchanges with the senior French commanders at Hartford Washington was focused on the capture of New York City.

Through his aide and interpreter, the Marquis de Lafayette, Washington wrote to Rochambeau and Admiral de Ternay on 9 July 1780 that he desired a French naval assault on New York.[4] A day later Lafayette addressed another message, this time to Count de La Luzerne: *"if M. de Ternay can go inside the Hook ... General Washington is entirely decided in favor of New York."*[5]

Well aware of the dangers of shallow water, the vicissitudes of winds and tides, to say nothing of the Royal Navy squadron at anchor, Admiral de Ternay responded to Lafayette on 16 July 1780 that: *"it would be extremely difficult to enter Sandy Hook because of shallow water."*[6]

Alexander Hamilton also reported this same information to Washington. Hamilton had been Liaison Officer on board Admiral d'Estaing's flagship when soundings off Sandy Hook were taken in 1778.

---

3 Washington spoke not a word of French; Rochambeau and de Ternay spoke no English. Therefore, the only man who could bring about the vital exchange of letters at this time was Lafayette. Chernow, p. 12.

4 Idzerda, Vol. III, pp. 69-76. Three of de Ternay's seven ships at Newport were 74-gun ships-of-the-line with 27-foot drafts. Comparable British ships drew 22-24 feet of water.

5 Idzerda, Vol. III, pp. 76-77.

6 Idzerda, Vol. III, pp. 96-97.

On 22 July 1780 Washington acknowledged de Ternay's frank appraisal of the obstacles and, ever the realist, adjusted his thinking accordingly. It is possible that it was at this time that Washington recognized that New York was beyond his grasp and that a more suitable target should be sought.

> I have received my dear Marquis your letter of the 20th inclosing me those you had received from Count de Rochambeau and The Chevalier de Ternay. As I speak to you in confidence I am sorry to find that the objections made by Mr. de Ternay are of a nature to prevent his entering the harbour notwithstanding any superiority he will probably have. I certainly would not wish him to endanger his fleet in any enterprise not warranted by prudence and by a sufficient prospect of success and security; and I shall acquiesce in his better judgment of Maritime Affairs. But I should hope whenever *if* he had a decided superiority he might possess the port, and certainly without this our operations must be infinitely more precarious, and in success much less decisive.[7]

Shallow water at Sandy Hook was a definite and valid concern. British charts made in 1766 and 1782 show 3.5 fathoms (21 feet) at low tide. In a letter sent to the Admiralty on 8 October 1779, Admiral Marriot Arbuthnot stated that *"at spring tides there is generally thirty feet of water on the [Sandy Hook] bar at high water."*[8]

---

7 Idzerda, Vol. III, pp. 105-107 (extract of Washington's letter)

8 Idzerda, Vol. III, p. 26; John Montresor "A plan of the City of New York 1766"; and John Hills, "A Chart of the Bar off Sandy Hook 1782" in the Library of Congress on-line map collection. The French navy obtained this information in July 1778 when Admiral d'Estaing maneuvered briefly off Sandy Hook. The French might also have obtained British soundings courtesy of the highly effective American spy networks operating in New York.

**Depth of water at Sandy Hook Bar**
Least Water (lowest low tide)    20 to 21 feet
Mean High Tide    25 to 27 feet
Spring Tides (highest high tide)    28 to 30 feet

**Ship Drafts**
French 74-Gun Ship    27 feet
British 74-Gun Ship    22 to 24 feet

Given their information concerning the tides, the French had serious doubts about their ability to navigate the shallow water of the channel by Sandy Hook in view of the 27-foot draft of their ships-of-the-line.[9]

But there is another special feature of the Sandy Hook bar. While larger French ships might have been able to *enter* New York harbor at the highest high tide accompanied by a strong onshore wind – once inside the harbor *they would be effectively trapped as the water level fell until the next highest high tide two weeks later.* The onshore wind also is significant because the wind piles up the water in the channel, thus causing the water to attain a depth of thirty feet at highest high tide.[10] Hence, larger ships could enter

---

9 Ship draft sources: March to Victory, p. 11; The Battle for New York, p. 312; Richard M. Ketchum, Victory at Yorktown, pp. 138-139, 169. "Spring" tides, a nautical term of art, describes exceptional tides created twice monthly when the gravitational pull of the sun and moon reinforce each other.

10 A tide table based on observations made in 1834 and published on a New York Bay and Harbor chart showed that at Least Water, there was between 20 and 21 feet of depth, at Spring Tides between 28 and 30 feet, and the Mean High Tide was 26-27 feet. Spring Tides occur only when the sun and moon align. In addition to information supplied him by the French and by Hamilton, Washington would have been fully aware of the water depths from his own collection of maps. See Barnet Schecter, George Washington's America, a biography through his maps, page 126 (map 29) containing an inset "A Chart of the Entrance to New York

and depart through the channel only at certain times of the month. This limitation is not conducive to naval operations.

Although the shallow water greatly raised the risks and difficulties of maneuvering deep-draft ships into New York harbor, the water alone was not the only danger facing the French. The Royal Navy had crossed the Sandy Hook bar in July 1776 to land troops on Staten Island and then proceeded to invest the port unmolested since the Americans had no naval forces to prevent them from doing so.

However, in July 1780 the situation in New York harbor was entirely different. In 1780 the Royal Navy had a permanent presence there. Thus, the potential danger of shallow water when combined with the certainty of fierce British naval resistance (supplemented by artillery fire from shore batteries) would make a French entry into New York harbor extremely hazardous. Not least, even if the French were able to overwhelm and defeat the Royal Navy squadron at New York, a second powerful British fleet could easily blockade the harbor, trapping the French ships at low tide, and then bring on a general engagement that would be disastrous to the French.

It is therefore possible that as early as July 1780, but certainly by the time of the Hartford meeting in September, doubts began to arise in Washington's mind about the feasibility of an investment of New York City by sea.

Adding to these considerations was the fact that Washington was painfully aware that superior numbers of land forces were required if an assault on New York was to be successful. First, as supreme headquarters of the British command in America, New York was heavily garrisoned. As noted, Sir Henry had for his defense some ten thousand troops, plus artillery – in prepared positions. For an assault to be carried out with any prospect of success, the French and Americans would need at least double that number of soldiers. Where would Washington come up with such a number? Together,

---

from Sandy Hook" on "A Plan of the City of New-York and its Environs" (1775).

Washington and Rochambeau had between them perhaps roughly the same number of soldiers as did Sir Henry Clinton.

Finally, Manhattan is an island. After nearly four years of British occupation, it might be said that New York was a *heavily fortified* island. The French and American planners were well aware that an assault would require an amphibious landing – against opposition – and that would be very costly indeed. On the water there would be no possibility of concealment or cover, and the element of surprise – if any existed at all, given Sir Henry's own highly effective network of spies and informers – was doubtful. Assault boats would be sitting ducks for British naval vessels, shore-based artillery and, at closer quarters, for British marksmen and massed fire from prepared positions on Manhattan.

One other consideration weighed into the equation. Because New York was not only an island but a major seaport like Charleston, a successful investment of the city could only be accomplished with fire support from naval forces. In the case of Charleston – where there had been no American or French naval force to fend off Admiral Arbuthnot – Sir Henry could depend on the presence of a Royal Navy squadron to surround and bombard Benjamin Lincoln in May 1780. But in fall 1780 there was virtually no possibility of a French fleet surrounding or bombarding Sir Henry Clinton in New York.

Perhaps the Franco-American planners had considered the possibility of surrounding and starving out the British garrison. True, a garrison requires substantial quantities of food each day, plus the usual medicines, repair parts, clothing, and other items. But New York was well stocked with all the provisions and supplies that Sir Henry deemed necessary. And a campaign designed to starve out the British defenders could take months, perhaps years. Moreover, such a plan would require the presence of a substantial French fleet for quite a prolonged period.

There were three problems with conducting a lengthy siege of New York. First, the Royal Navy would undoubtedly try to break a French blockade by bringing on a general engagement off Sandy Hook. Second, the British held the opinion (probably correctly) that the French navy could not leave the French West Indies unprotected. Third, weather conditions affect all navies, but the French admirals appeared to be more sensitive to the advent of hurricane season and unfavorable winds than the British. The British also assumed that the Royal Navy would maintain naval superiority along the Atlantic coast, perhaps in part because they outnumbered the French vessels and in part because their ships-of-the-line were more seaworthy. In any case, the British believed their seamanship was superior to the French. (It is possible that secretly the French naval officers may have held the same opinion.)

Taking all these factors together, it is more than probable that Washington, Rochambeau, Admiral de Ternay, and Lafayette concluded that New York was beyond their reach. An assault might well carry the day if the French and Americans could raise the requisite number of soldiers, but an amphibious landing was highly risky and a frontal assault would be extremely costly in lives. A naval investment against fierce resistance was impractical, especially given the risky situation with winds and tides. *What would be the result if the American and French land forces, even if successful, suffered the same scale of casualties assaulting New York as they had suffered at Savannah in Fall 1779? What if the French fleet were defeated, destroyed or merely driven away by a concentration of British naval power off Long Island? Given the objective factors, what was the probability of success or failure? Was New York really worth the high risks involved?*

After their first exchange of letters in July 1780, and leading up to the Hartford meeting in September, Washington and the French commanders almost certainly had spent much time and effort studying the feasibility of attacking New York. By the fall of 1780 it must have become painfully obvious that the required mix of land and naval forces for a successful amphibious assault on New York simply could not be mustered.

There was one final most discouraging consideration. Even if Washington *could* re-take New York (with French naval help) he would be unable to *hold* the city. The French fleet would be withdrawn for service in Europe or the West Indies, leaving the Americans once again naked to a Royal Navy attack and landing just as they had been in 1776.[11]

The planners now evaluated the costs and risks attendant to an engagement in the South. During the summer of 1780, the forces under Lord Cornwallis were still on the strategic offensive in the Carolinas – though, as mentioned, distance, time, and even "victory" was taking its toll on his forces. The number of Cornwallis' effective troops was steadily dwindling the farther he advanced. Even had not King's Mountain and Cowpens cost Lord Cornwallis nearly 2,000 soldiers – soldiers he could replace only with difficulty – it is likely that disease, malnutrition, fatigue, and desertion would have worn his forces down.[12] Added to this attrition was Cornwallis' need to leave detachments behind to attempt to hold strategic points such as Ninety-Six that had fallen into his hands. Cornwallis was stretching himself very thin, perhaps dangerously so.

The British had not yet invaded Virginia. Thus, Virginia did not become the main focus of allied operations until General Phillips

---

11 Many historians who lack military or intelligence experience fail to appreciate that once you have captured a position, you then must defend it against counterattack. This may explain why these scholars too readily swallow Washington's "plan" to seize New York as being his true objective after the Hartford meeting. Washington was only too familiar with the strategic realities he faced in assaulting New York. He knew, if the historians did not, that the key to victory was to break the enemy's will to fight – not to capture fixed points. Rather than staging a costly and sanguinary frontal assault on a city he knew he could not hold – should he capture it – Washington knew that to break Britain's will to fight, he had to trap and destroy a vulnerable enemy army in the field. That meant destroying either Phillips or Cornwallis.

12 British Major General Leslie had occupied Portsmouth in October 1780, but was withdrawn by Lord Cornwallis when Leslie's troops were needed to help replenish British losses at King's Mountain.

arrived in March 1781 followed by Cornwallis in May. Phillips' command was significantly larger than that under Cornwallis. But even if the two forces should combine, they would nevertheless be vulnerable to attack by a more powerful Franco-American land force supported by sea power.

It is safe to say that Charleston would have been an attractive and relatively safe allied target with Cornwallis mired deep in the wilds of North Carolina. True, the capture of Charleston, or even Portsmouth into the bargain, would not have had the same political impact either in Great Britain or America as would the seizure of New York City. True also that victory over relatively small garrisons in South Carolina would not break the back of the British army in America. Destruction of a major British field army, however, would at one stroke achieve both the military and political ends sought.

Thus, the practical possibility of success appeared far more likely in some southern location than at New York. What is more, victory could be achieved with far fewer resources – and much less risk of loss – than would be needed were New York the target. Put simply, a decisive allied victory was more probable in the South than in the North.

Victory at Charleston would cancel the effect, politically and psychologically, of Sir Henry's May 1780 triumph. Loss of Charleston also would imperil Cornwallis' already tenuous lines of communication and, in any event, would encourage the Patriot forces while dampening Tory hopes. Had the Franco-American allies seized Charleston, their subsequent goal would have been to destroy all British forces and garrisons in Georgia and the Carolinas – all of which were dependent upon Charleston for supplies.[13]

---

13 In effect, such a campaign, starting from Charleston, would have had the same effect as did Nathanael Greene's 1781 campaign moving against the British garrisons from the north. However, it should be borne in mind that these scattered British garrisons, such as those at Camden and Ninety Six, constituted fully 20% of Sir Henry Clinton's total land forces. But by being scattered, they were of little strategic value.

Moreover, just possibly, a convincing American triumph in the South – however modest – might help bring down Lord North's politically vulnerable government.

Yet another factor that must have appealed to the French was the fact that Charleston is several hundred miles nearer the West Indies than is New York City – thus allowing for a relatively shorter movement of the fleet. Not least, the Royal Navy's presence in the South after Sir Henry's return to New York was palpably thin. Local naval superiority could be gained and held by the French more easily off Charleston than off Long Island.

Now, the allied plans staff also must have been aware of some negative aspects to this move. First, the Franco-American armies would have to move overland from the Hudson Valley to the South – they lacked "canvas wings" of their own. A movement overland would be arduous and slow, even if the armies were not opposed by hostile forces and even if those forces were aided and assisted by Patriot civilians. Also, troops on the move are more subject to the vicissitudes of movement – accidents, sickness, loss by desertion, and the constant need for supplies, especially food.

The other key planning factor, indeed the decisive factor, was the question mark concerning the possibility of local superiority at sea. If even temporary French command of the sea could be gained, a British expeditionary force dependent on a logistical tail could be trapped and beaten – even starved into surrender. But if temporary allied command of the sea could not be achieved, British forces could be reinforced…or if need be, extracted by the Royal Navy and transported elsewhere swiftly and safely. Thus, the major unknown in the allied planners' calculations was the ability of a powerful French fleet to move unopposed into American waters and cut off the southern British army from any hope of rescue or reinforcement.

Ultimately, the Franco-American considerations boiled down to these: *Would British expeditionary forces in the South be reduced in number and effectiveness to render them sufficiently vulnerable to a weak (but still relatively more powerful) allied force? Could French naval power blockade part of the southern coast, even temporarily, thus severing Cornwallis' contact with the Royal Navy? How could the Franco-American army be moved from New York to the South without alerting the ever-vigilant Sir Henry Clinton?*

Given this line of thinking, it is possible – even likely – that the conferees at Hartford in September 1780 had decided upon a bold strike at British forces in the American South. Clearly there were risks and unknowns to this strategy. But by the same token, victory appeared far more likely in the South than around New York.

If this decision was taken at Hartford in late September 1780, then what remained was to arrange for French naval support when the security situation in the West Indies would permit and the prevailing winds were favorable; to prepare the Franco-American armies for the decisive moment and, above all, to deceive Sir Henry Clinton. And also, for good measure, it was necessary for Washington to deceive his fellow Americans.

# IX

# WASHINGTON'S CONFESSION

Seven years after Cornwallis' surrender at Yorktown, in response to a question posed by the eminent man-of-letters, Noah Webster, Washington wrote a remarkable letter about certain details of the Revolution. Washington's letter, written in July 1788, is almost a "confessional." The letter is so important to understanding how the British were defeated that it is quoted in full.

As the war neared its end, Washington's appraisal of the strategic situation and his few options rested on two key considerations. First, Washington well knew the niggardly ways of the state legislatures and their reluctance to provide any resources, military or otherwise, for his use much beyond their state borders. As we have seen, in Washington's view it was equally, if not more important to mislead his "friends" in Albany, Boston, or Hartford, or even his own staff, as it was his British foe, Sir Henry Clinton. Had he openly declared his intention to strike at some point other than New York, it is doubtful that much manpower or treasure would have been forthcoming from New England.

Second, as a spymaster of the first order, Washington was well aware that his British foes had penetrated his own command with their own spies. He knew that Tory sympathizers kept his forces under constant surveillance and that British intelligence officers such as Major John Andre could place trained agents in or near his most sensitive installations. Indeed, historian John Bakeless, discussing Sir Henry's need to "vet" the would-be traitor Benedict Arnold prior to accepting him as a defector, asked Major Andre to carry out this work secretly.

> Clinton soon had so many well-trained secret agents in New York that he could hurry spies out to investigate, the moment a query came in. Andre, for example, at one time became suspicious that Arnold did not really mean to turn traitor, but was only leading the British on. The major's assistant, Joseph Chew, was able to "put two persons out in order to obtain an account of Mr. [Benedict] Arnold's movements," *within two and a half hours.*[1]

Or again, as noted by historian Rupert Hughes:

> He [Washington] was not able even to bring off a little attempt to kidnap General Knyphausen or Clinton, on Christmas night [ed. 1780]. The careful plan he agreed on with Colonel Humphreys was disclosed by a spy in camp. Clinton knew all about it, and responded with plots to kidnap Washington, which were likewise carried to him by spies in Clinton's camp.[2]

Washington was under no illusion that whatever gambit he conceived, it would quickly come to Sir Henry's attention.

In addition to British spies, there was also the very real concern that "loose lips" among his friends and allies might sink his plans. If Washington were to discuss his plans with more than a very few trusted – and highly circumspect – men, he knew that sooner or

---

1 Bakeless, p. 268. Italics added for emphasis.

2 Hughes, p. 585. The unsung Irish-American hero, Hercules Mulligan, then a tailor in Occupied New York, is credited with tipping off Washington to Clinton's plot.

later the information would leak out and become known to his opponents.

Adding to this concern was the ever-present possibility of loss of vital documents to the enemy. If Washington could capture the diaries, papers, and dispatches of British officers, was it not equally possible for his enemies to capture some of his own papers? What if the British intelligence officers should obtain a copy of a grand strategic plan they concluded was genuine pointing to a major American move into the South?

The need for total secrecy -- on a par with that exercised by the Anglo-American Allies in World War II in protecting "Ultra" and Overlord, complete with tightly controlled "bigot lists" – was absolutely imperative.[3] In July 1788 Washington described much of this to Noah Webster:[4]

> Mount Vernon, July 31, 1788.
>
> Sir: I duly received your letter of the 14th. instant, and can only answer very *briefly*, and generally from *memory*: that a combined operation of the land and naval forces of France in America, for the year 1781, *was preconcerted the year before*: that the point of attack was not absolutely agreed upon, because it would be easy for the Count de Grasse, in good time before his departure from the West Indies, to give notice by Express, at what place he could most conveniently first touch to receive advice, because it could not be foreknown where the enemy would be most susceptible of impression; and because we (having the command of the water with sufficient means of conveyance) could transport ourselves to any spot with the greatest celerity: that it was determined by me (nearly twelve months beforehand) at all hazards to give out and cause it to be believed by the highest military as well as civil Officers that

---

3 A "bigot list" is a term of art in the intelligence world that describes those few and carefully selected individuals who have been approved for access to highly sensitive intelligence.

4 WGW: Fk, Vol. 30, pages 26-28.

New York was the destined place of attack, for the important purpose of inducing the Eastern and Middle States to make greater exertions in furnishing specific supplies than they otherwise would have done, as well as for the interesting purpose of rendering the enemy less prepared elsewhere: that, by these means and these alone, artillery, Boats, Stores and Provisions were in seasonable preparation to move with the utmost rapidity to any part of the Continent; for the difficulty consisted more in providing, than knowing how to apply the military apparatus: that before the arrival of the Count de Grasse it was the fixed determination to *strike the enemy in the most vulnerable quarter* so as to ensure success with moral certainty, as our affairs were then in the most ruinous train imaginable: that New York was thought to be beyond our effort and consequently the only hesitation that remained was between an attack upon the British army in Virginia or that in Charleston: and finally that (by the intervention of several communications and some incidents which cannot be Detailed in a letter; and wch. were *altogether unknown* to the late Quartermaster General of the Army,[5] who was informed of nothing but what related to the immediate duties of his own department) the hostile Post in Virginia, from being a *provisional and strongly expected* became the *definitive and certain object* of the Campaign. I only add, that it never was in contemplation to attack New York, unless the Garrison should first have been so far disgarnished to carry on the southern operations, as to render our success in the siege of that place as infallible as any future military event can ever be made.[6] For

---

5 Timothy Pickering (1745-1829,) appointed by Congress on 5 August 1780 to succeed Nathanael Greene as Quartermaster General, was reported to have done an outstanding job despite meager resources. Colonel Pickering resigned as Quartermaster General on 25 July 1785 and went on to a distinguished public career in both federal and Massachusetts state service. Timothy Pickering along with his brother, John, was a close friend of Noah Webster. John Pickering assisted Webster with his famed dictionary.

6 On 14 July 1788 Webster had written to Washington: "The late Quarter Master General [Pickering] has assured me that a combined attack was intended to be made upon New York, and that the arrival of the French

I repeat it, and dwell upon it again and again, some splendid advantage (whether upon a larger or smaller scale was almost immaterial) was so essentially necessary to revive the expiring hopes and languid exertions of the Country, at the crisis in question, that I never would have consented to embark in any enterprize; wherein, from the most rational plan and accurate calculations, the favourable issue should not have appeared as clear to my view, as a ray of light. The failure of an attempt agst. the Posts of the enemy, could, in no other possible situation during the war, have been so fatal to our cause.

That much trouble was taken and finesse used to misguide and bewilder Sir Henry Clinton in regard to the real object, by fictitious communications, as well as by making a deceptive provision of Ovens, Forage and Boats in his Neighborhood, is certain. Nor were less pains taken to deceive our own Army; for I had always conceived, when the imposition did not completely take place at home, it could never sufficiently succeed abroad.

Your desire of obtaining truth is very laudable, I wish I had more leizure (sic) to gratify it: as I am equally solicitous the undisguised verity should be known. Many circumstances will unavoidably be misconceived and misrepresented. Notwithstanding most of the Papers which may properly be deemed official are preserved; yet the knowledge of innumerable things, of a more delicate and secret nature, is confined to the perishable remembrance of some few of the present generation. With esteem I am.

Geo. Washington

Perhaps in no other single document can so much of Washington's strategic genius and his deep understanding of men and human nature be seen. In this letter Washington lays out not only his

---

fleet in the Bay of Chesapeak was unexpected, and changed the plan of operations." [Letter in the *Washington Papers*.] Col. Pickering was aware only of the cover story that New York was the target. Washington makes the point: *"[Pickering] was informed of nothing but what related to the immediate duties of his own department."* WGW: Fk, page 27, Note.

appraisal of his "friends" and foes, but how he intended to play what cards he held. And Washington knew that he had few cards to play – perhaps the most valuable card being his ability to bluff his chief adversary, Sir Henry Clinton.

Washington's biographers routinely conclude that Washington was lock-set on assaulting New York City until shortly before heading for Yorktown. Indeed, that is precisely the impression Washington wished to give his British adversaries (a goal he achieved.) As it happens, many historians also have fallen for his ruse. Therefore, most histories give the picture of Washington focusing all his energy on capturing Manhattan until abruptly changing his plans in mid-August 1781. Washington probably would be highly amused by this.

But Washington's actions show a very different picture from his words. Indeed, it is hard to explain how an experienced officer so wise and wily as George Washington could be so cavalier with his words, well knowing that in hours – or even minutes – Sir Henry would "hear" them. And possibly from several sources! As events were to prove, Washington was cavalier only in spreading humbug about. As for his real plans, he was the soul of discretion.

Washington's letter to Noah Webster twice refers to a strategic concept being agreed upon as early as fall 1780. Washington wrote that: *"a combined operation of the land and naval forces of France in America, for the year 1781, was preconcerted the year before..."* and later in the same letter: *"that it was determined by me (nearly twelve months beforehand) at all hazards to give out and cause it to be believed by the highest military as well as civil Officers that New York was the destined place of attack, for the important purpose of inducing the Eastern and Middle States to make greater exertions in furnishing specific supplies than they otherwise would have done, as well as for the interesting purpose of rendering the enemy less prepared elsewhere..."* If we may take Washington at his word, these two excerpts indicate that fully a year before Yorktown, almost certainly at the Hartford conference, plans were made to trap or destroy the

British army somewhere in the South, using threats against New York as a smokescreen to baffle *both* the British and the Americans.

True, the exact place for the denouement was left unspecified. But then, at the time the French were conferring with Washington at Hartford, Cornwallis was sweeping through the South, constantly on the move and heading steadily northward. Today we would consider what the senior allied commanders had conceptualized at Hartford to be a "contingency plan" with some key details necessarily left blank until the circumstances permitted those details to be penned in to the plan. In October 1780 not even Cornwallis himself envisioned – or could have envisioned – taking up a defensive position on the banks of the York River in Virginia. But Washington and Rochambeau considered that, sooner or later, logistical realities would render vulnerable the British southern army. Their plan was thus to be prepared to move at once "on order" the moment conditions were ripe.

Certain historians discount Washington's "confession" to Noah Webster as fabrication or, at best, the product of a confused and forgetful mind. The answer to this criticism is to be found in George Washington's character and in his later performance as America's first President. If his critics hope to discredit what Washington told Webster in July 1788 about the formulation of strategy in late 1780 – that his letter either was claptrap or the wandering of a failing memory – they must first impeach Washington's impressive powers of thought and judgment as the nation's Commander in Chief from 1789 to 1797. Since they cannot do this, we must therefore accept Washington's letter to Webster at its face value – as the truth.

Perhaps the genesis of the view that Washington's letter to Webster concerning his great deception was a lie stems from Timothy Pickering's comments to Benjamin Rush some years after the Revolution.

In 1791 Pickering told Rush, with some vehemence, that Washington's 1788 letter to Noah Webster, was a "lie." He went on to say that the letter would do great damage to Washington's reputation as a truthful man, and that it was absolutely impossible to believe that Washington had used the New York operation as a mere deception. Rush stated: *"Pickering explained and descended into particulars. He said it was false in Washington to pretend that he had meditated beforehand to deceive the enemy and in that end to deceive the officers and soldiers of his own army, [and] that he had seriously meditated an attack on New York for near a twelvemonth and had made preparations at enormous expense for that purpose. Washington never had a thought of marching to the southward, till the Count de Grasse's fleet appeared upon the coast [ed. 30 August 1781]. He knew it, Washington knew it; consequently that letter was a great disgrace."*

What must be understood is that Pickering, like any other member of Washington's staff, was subject to the "need to know" principle. Pickering therefore knew only the cover story designed to protect from compromise the Franco-American operation against Cornwallis. Perhaps Pickering was miffed that he had not been admitted into the secret or possibly he truly believed to the end that New York was the real target. Whatever Pickering's personal feelings, it is now clear that Washington's letter to Webster was the unvarnished truth. Pickering and those historians who believe that Washington's letter is a "lie" are simply wrong.[7]

The fact that George Washington and key staff began moving south to Virginia on 14-15 August 1781 to join Lafayette, with the main French and American armies following on 19 August (ten days before the French fleet had even anchored in Chesapeake) amply demonstrates that Washington well knew that the final act of the Revolution was at hand.

George Washington needs no witness to testify to the truthfulness of his statements. Yet, if the skeptics require it, testimony to the decisions made at Hartford – the decisions that shaped allied

---

7 See The Spur of Fame: Dialogues of John Adams and Benjamin Rush, 1805-1813; John A. Schatz and Douglas Adair, eds.; San Marino, CA 1966; pp. 212-213

operations in 1781 – comes from one unimpeachable witness. Lafayette.

On 4 October 1780, following the Hartford conference, Lafayette wrote to the Count de Vergennes the following letter, here extracted:

> Without naval superiority, Monsieur le Comte, there can be no sure operation in America. If the 4,000 men and seven ships [ed. under Rochambeau and Adm. de Ternay] had arrived early in spring, New York would have been ours, and we could have carried out successful operations against that place if, after Graves's arrival, M. de Guichen had come to help us. General Washington had no doubt about the advisability of attacking New York. If, in the course of this autumn, if say, two months from now, we achieve naval superiority, we could move against Charleston and regain the southern states. If, on the other hand, the British remain in command of the sea, we shall have to restrict ourselves to awaiting attacks, many of which will be difficult to fend off. Everyone will report to you, Monsieur le Comte, that Admiral Rodney arrived here with ten ships and that the British now have nineteen ships of the line in these waters, the importance of which they know very well. The second division causes us much anxiety as its delay occasions impatience in us and doubts among the Americans. When I returned to this continent I found the prejudices much abated; they are even more so recently, and my plan was to propose to you, not merely as a useful project but as an essential one, to open the next campaign here in early spring with a corps of ten thousand men and naval superiority assured. The situation of America demands your most serious attention; each year of delay increases the quantity of ships, men, and money you will have to send. If help had arrived early, if we had had naval superiority, next year's [ed. 1781] increase would have become unnecessary.
>
> M. de Ternay's seven ships are keeping nineteen of theirs occupied, and considering this fact, one cannot say they are useless. The French division has rescued us from a very dangerous offensive that General Clinton was obliged to abandon. The division has provided us with a pretext to alert the states and obtain troops, and its outstanding conduct has

created a high opinion of our national discipline. But that is not enough, Monsieur le Comte, and under the circumstances, in the position America is in, it is essential to the interest as well as the honor of France that our flag rule over these waters, that the campaign be decisive, and that it begin next spring.

A few days ago, Monsieur le Comte, General Washington and I returned from Hartford, where we had a meeting with the French generals. General Washington's opinion is wholly reported in the resume, an extract of which the king's minister has sent you. They decided by common consent what should be done in either of the two following circumstances: that in which we should attain maritime superiority this autumn and that in which our inferiority would continue. *In the first case we would embark on the Delaware four thousand men, who, joined to four thousand French and having picked up about two thousand men in the South, where the cavalry would be sent by land, would enable us, with the help of the militia, to regain South Carolina and Georgia.* After the first of January, there would be remaining here the Continental garrison of West Point supported by the militia.

In the second case they decided that nothing could be done and we should busy ourselves with the next campaign. The French generals made proposals to General Washington that the commander in chief could only approve. These requests and the answers to them will be the basis of a memoir the French generals will send you by frigate.[8]

Hartford set the grand strategy, and the centerpiece of that strategy was gaining full command of the sea. It is clear that liberation of the American South was of central importance to the allied commanders. They knew that New York was beyond their reach.

---

8 Extracts of Lafayette's letter to Comte de Vergennes, 4 October 1780. Idzerda, Vol. III, pp. 188-190. Italics added for emphasis. The nearly three-to-one British advantage over the French in capital ships, combined with the peculiar nature of the shallow waters off Sandy Hook, eliminated New York in 1780 as being a viable target for any possible Franco-American amphibious assault.

# X

# Washington's Sound and Light Show

So how did Sir Henry fall into the net? What factors caused him to accept as true what was patently false?

As noted, when ingrained habits of thinking begin to take shape, they tend to admit those bits of information that conform to the established patterns and to exclude or lock out any conflicting information. Indeed, as noted, some otherwise obvious and easily observed acts or events become invisible.

Sir Henry became a prisoner of his own cognitive faults because of the following:

Like many senior British generals, Sir Henry Clinton tended to view Americans as "mere provincials" who, with very few exceptions, were incapable of any degree of soldierly discipline or professionalism comparable to officers of the great European states. Indeed, in 1755 General Edward Braddock openly looked down on American "provincials" as having nothing worthy of his attention. This attitude in no small measure contributed to Braddock's undoing in western Pennsylvania. General James Wolfe, victor at Quebec in 1759, also held a particularly low opinion of Americans. He is quoted as remarking that American militiamen were *"...in general, the dirtiest most contemptible, cowardly dogs you can conceive."*[1]

Lord George Germain, Clinton's immediate superior in London, is alleged to have said the following about Americans: *"...the rabble ... ought not trouble themselves with politics and government, which they do not understand."* and that *"...these country clowns cannot whip us."*[2]

Clinton almost certainly agreed with the vast majority of his colleagues – except perhaps the Howe brothers – that the American rebels were cowardly and naïve, barely capable of only the most rudimentary political and military activities. Sir Henry's preconceived notion about Americans was therefore his first step toward self-deception.

Moreover, given his experience since 1776, Sir Henry believed that Americans could not keep secrets secret. Inevitably, there would be a leak or some other breach of security that would reveal even the "most secret" plans. It is a fact that Clinton relied for a great share of his basic intelligence on the typical American propensity to brag or merely trade idle gossip. Like Antonia Ford or Belle Boyd in the American Civil War – Confederate spies who charmed many Union officers into confiding sometimes highly sensitive information – all Sir Henry had to do to obtain valuable nuggets was simply have a sympathetic pair of Tory ears in a drawing room, tavern, tailor's shop, or officer's billet. Indeed, Washington himself had just such a valuable pair of Patriot ears in British New York -- the humble Irish-American tailor, Hercules Mulligan.[3] Sometimes

---

1 Kennedy, <u>The American Pageant</u>, Vol. I; pages 117, 121. Tuchman [op. cit., p. 145] adds to General Wolfe's comment: *"...rather an encumbrance than any real strength to an army."*

2 Quoted at http://www.enotes.com/topic/George_Germain,_1st_Viscount_Sackville.

3 Bakeless, p. 240. This is not to neglect the Culper Ring and many other valuable American spies.

even the "highly professional" British officers liked to brag or strut their importance, giving away valuable information.

Not least, Sir Henry Clinton was a prisoner of his own extensive experience. As a lieutenant general with years of field experience in Europe and America, he was well acquainted with how armies function. Sir Henry could observe a part of an enemy force and, based upon his own knowledge of military forces, pretty well calculate that unit's troop strength, armament, line of march, and even the caliber of the soldiers ranged against him. If he could do this with French or German units – all of them infinitely superior to the ragtag rebels – how much easier, thought Sir Henry, with Americans?

Modern military G-2 sections use a technique that is similar in many ways to Sir Henry's less formal method. It is called "templating." When certain units or weapons are spotted on the battlefield, these "hits" are plotted on a tactical map at headquarters. Then, based upon known enemy doctrine – and past experience – combat intelligence officers can deduce where other units or weapons are most likely to be hidden. "Templating" is thus a kind of military algebra – one uses known quantities to find other, unknown quantities. A commander might then send out a patrol or, if he has aircraft, fly over the areas where the G-2 suspects the hidden units or weapons will be found.

Even in his day, Sir Henry could use a number of similar "metrics" to gauge the strength and intentions of an enemy. He would consider the number of campfires counted, the number of soldiers seen marching, flags and pendants observed, and certainly all manner of logistical preparations reported such as supply wagons, bake ovens, tents of various kinds, water and food storage depots, and so on. Even Sir Henry's most skeptical intelligence officers would take into account the fact that so many key "metrics" had been reported – sightings they could plot on the situation map for their commander.

From sightings and from agent reports, Sir Henry and his staff could begin to compile a "picture" of French and American dispositions and troop movements. "Templating" could be used to deduce where other units or supply points, presently unobserved, might be found. What Clinton most desired was information on Franco-American "plans and intentions." He knew that deployments in the field and tactical plans had to match.

But perhaps the most salient feature of all was Sir Henry's readiness to believe that *his* force was Washington's target. *After all, wasn't New York City Great Britain's supreme headquarters in the colonies? Wasn't his the most important garrison in America? And wasn't he the most significant British commander?* While not making too much of Sir Henry's ego, it nonetheless probably colored his judgment at least subconsciously. Whatever good things for His Majesty that Generals Phillips, Cornwallis or Arnold might do in the Carolinas or Virginia, Sir Henry firmly believed that what really mattered was what *he* did in New York.

We might surmise that well before late 1780 Washington had taken the measure of Sir Henry Clinton and had come to understand his British adversary very well indeed.

The American supreme commander probably knew Clinton's predilections regarding "mere provincials" and the British commander's preconceived ideas regarding American capabilities, tactical or otherwise. Why not play on these prejudices?

Washington was certainly under no illusion whatsoever that his own headquarters leaked like a sieve and, in any case, was penetrated by clever British spies. Accepting this reality for what it was, Washington took advantage of the "loose lips" atmosphere to float all manner of rumors and gossip, well knowing that all this humbug would speedily find its way to Sir Henry – and some of it would be believed.

Despite Sir Henry's myopia regarding America and its inhabitants, Washington fully appreciated that Clinton was an intelligent man and had many years of experience in the field. Sir Henry was anything but a rube. This being the case, as a master impresario, Washington arranged his well-set stage to be seen (or "detected") by Clinton's spies and by Sir Henry in person. Everything would be there. But everything was a "Potemkin Village" or, if you prefer, a Hollywood storefront.

And perhaps, just perhaps, Washington had come to understand that General Clinton viewed himself – and "his" city – as being the unquestioned center of the British counterinsurgency effort in America. Sir Henry probably thought that control of America depended on control of New York; in turn, as British supreme commander, he controlled New York. All other theaters of operation were subsidiaries of supreme headquarters. Sir Henry's flash of ego was a key psychological vulnerability, and Washington knew it.

Given a clear picture of his chief adversary, and the mindset of Clinton's principal staff officers and advisors, perhaps aided by insights supplied by Rivington and others, Washington thereupon set out to show Sir Henry what Sir Henry wanted to see. Starting as early as the Fall of 1780 Washington began his campaign aimed at stage-managing events around New York to lull the British commander into a misplaced sense of importance…while carefully distorting Sir Henry's view of reality.

For many months prior to the October 1781 showdown at Yorktown, Washington did a masterful job of manipulating his enemy's perception of reality – while preparing the ground for his later masterstroke. In effect, Washington pulled off a "double deception." Not only did he reinforce Sir Henry's pre-existing belief that New York was to be the Americans' target, *but he also persuaded both Clinton and Cornwallis that the South was of no military interest.*

> Confuse your enemy; make your opponent believe you are going to do what you aren't, and then convince him you will not do what you intend.[4]

---

4 Lamborn, <u>The People in Arms</u>, p. 101.

Washington's feat of legerdemain was to prove fatal for British rule in America.

The central question to be pondered, however, is why Sir Henry chose to underestimate George Washington. Sir Henry Clinton had arrived in America in May 1775. Of all British senior officers in America, he had had the longest service and therefore the greatest opportunity to take the measure of his American adversary. Time and again a militarily weak Washington had pulled the wool over the eyes of various British and Hessian commanders having superior forces. Washington had proved himself wily and imaginative. Why was Sir Henry Clinton so slow to recognize his tall American adversary as a master of deception?

# XI

# Washington's Boffo Performance

Washington and his French cohorts understood that for a strategic deception of the British to have any chance of success, it must convincingly address two issues of universal importance to all military men: knowledge of *capabilities and intentions.*

Certainly knowledge of Franco-American capabilities and intentions was of highest importance to Sir Henry Clinton. The first of these was largely a matter of observation. Tory sympathizers who visited rebel camps, the testimony of secret agents and defectors, and Sir Henry's own spyglass would be sufficient to reckon the rebels' strength and dispositions – the capabilities of the Franco-American enemy forces ranged against him.

Reports came to Sir Henry about the marshaling of boats – definitely needed to mount an amphibious landing on Staten Island or Manhattan. Tories reported seeing French field bakeries being placed at various locations in what today would be called the "brigade trains area" – behind the maneuver areas needed by infantry, but close enough to support the troops. Supplies (or at least what might appear to be supplies) also would have to be gathered into depots near troop cantonments.

# Washington's Boffo Performance

The Abbe Claude Robin, chaplain of the French army, marveled at Washington's ability to make and unmake his Hollywood storefront:

> Now with a few soldiers he forms a Spacious Camp.... Then again with a large number of men he reduces his tentage and his force almost vanishes.[1]

Realizing in early June 1781 that the final drama of the American Revolution was about to be played, Washington and Rochambeau redoubled their efforts to build a deception that was to alarm Sir Henry Clinton. Very publicly, the French army commenced its move from its base at Newport – marching somewhat noisily from Rhode Island across Connecticut to join Washington's forces facing New York on 5 July 1781.[2] From late June until well into August, Washington and Rochambeau conducted joint maneuvers, scouted the defenses of New York, made logistical preparations, and made highly visible personal appearances with their troops as if they were finalizing preparations to lay siege to New York City. French and American units "on the march" undoubtedly were duly reported to Sir Henry Clinton by his diligent Tory snitches.

The noisy march was a sham, however, proven by the fact that the French left their heavy siege artillery and its ammunition behind in Newport. Only mortars and some field artillery pieces were taken along on the march to New York. Siege artillery would be required for the successful conduct of a siege – and it should have been taken to White Plains if the objective really had been New York.

---

1 Davis, p. 29

2 Even when combined, the Allied force was approximately 11,600 men – far too few to seriously menace New York City given that Clinton had a nearly equal number of men in strong prepared defensive positions and sufficient Royal Navy support to prevent a French investment of Manhattan from the sea.

The reason for this significant "lapse" – evidently missed by Sir Henry's spies at the time and by most historians later – is quite obvious: the French siege artillery was intended for operations in the Chesapeake, and would be conveyed there by Count de Barras in August. There would be no point in lugging heavy and cumbersome pieces of siege artillery overland only to have to re-deploy those same pieces back over the same Connecticut roads in a matter of a few weeks.[3] Moreover, transporting siege artillery by sea to Long Island Sound or the New Jersey coast would have been risky. Capture or destruction would have been easy for the Royal Navy or perhaps for a rapid British amphibious operation. Better to keep the precious (and perhaps irreplaceable) siege guns safe in Newport for eventual use in Virginia.

Not least, in July the Americans and French conducted several minor attacks on outlying defensive works around New York City, notably in the Kingsbridge Heights area north of Manhattan. These and other minor clashes were enough to keep Sir Henry's attention properly focused. Perhaps Clinton thought of these as preliminary probes meant to test his outer defenses prior to the full-scale assault he believed imminent. But neither Washington nor Rochambeau allowed these skirmishes to escalate into uncontrolled major battles.

Yes, there were certainly gaps in this tactical information, but the weight of evidence of growing allied capabilities near New York was clear enough to Sir Henry and his principal staff.

However, the most persistent area of doubt for a commander is, and probably will forever remain, gaining full knowledge of his enemy's plans and intentions.

True, the enemy's dispositions do provide clues to his intentions. But only very rough clues. Dispositions of troops and supporting elements do not speak to the vital questions of "when" and "how." On those key points, troop dispositions are mute.

---

3 So far as is known, no one at the time asked the question: *"But where is the siege artillery?"* Had this lapse been noted by a British intelligence officer, it might have exposed the operation as a deception.

What Sir Henry needed was an informant inside Washington's headquarters…or captured operational documentation…or preferably, both.

Intelligence officers seek "confirmation" of agent reporting. Even the most observant and faithful human sources cannot always report with 100% accuracy or completeness. They may have misheard information that was spoken as they eavesdropped. They may not have understood what they heard or saw. Perhaps they forgot some details – or failed to note vital details. Human sources are necessarily fallible due to their very humanity.

For this reason, intelligence officers only very rarely place credence in "single source" information. If there is nothing to "confirm" what is reported, then however reliable the source is, his report is considered "unconfirmed information" and accorded the healthy skepticism it may deserve. We have already heard from Clausewitz on the doubtfulness of intelligence obtained in war.

But if elements of a "single source" report are confirmed by other sources – independent of and unknown to that source – the analyst's initial skepticism begins to fade.

And when a report provided by an agent or informant is confirmed not merely by the reporting of others, but by what can be observed, and further by documentary evidence, that testimony becomes strong indeed. It takes on the character of "fact." This was, of course, the standard intelligence practice of all armies in the 18th century, and remains standard analytical practice to this day.

There is only one problem with this process. As observations, reports, and documents accumulate, all seeming to point in one direction, the "weight of evidence" tends to choke out any information that appears contradictory, at variance, or out-of-step with what is increasingly viewed as being "true."

Washington and his French allies wished that the "evidence" they provided was viewed by the British as being so weighty that Sir Henry would regard it as unimpeachable.[4]

Three years earlier, in the fall of 1777, Washington and his staff officers had pulled off a nearly identical strategic deception of the British. Indeed, it is probable that the experience gained at that time by the American side in duping General Howe and Sir Henry Clinton was put to good use in 1780.

Many historians point to the decisive American victory at Saratoga as the "turning point" of the American Revolution. Clearly, Saratoga paved the way for French recognition of the fledgling nation and a declaration of war against Great Britain.[5] While the assistance of France did not guarantee American independence, it cannot be denied that France's material, financial, and political aid made independence possible.

What is of nearly equal importance to the great victory, but less well known, is what took place immediately following "Gentleman Johnny" Burgoyne's surrender. Had Sir Henry Clinton been a bit more observant in 1777, he might at that time have taken careful note of the imaginative trickery and clever make-believe of which the American "country clowns" and "cowardly dogs" were capable.

---

4 Bakeless, p. 194, notes that Washington never overplayed his hand when deceiving his enemies. He knew that the success of an operation depended upon its credibility. His advice to his staff in formulating false materials: *"Keep it within the bounds of what may be thought reasonable or probable."*

5 George Washington wrote to Israel Putnam on 19 October 1777 (two days after Burgoyne surrendered, thus indicating a swift courier service to and from the front) as follows: *"The defeat of Genl. Burgoyne is a most important event, and such as must afford the highest satisfaction to every well affected American breast. Should providence be pleased to crown our Arms in the course of the Campaign, with one more fortunate stroke, I think we shall have no great cause for anxiety respecting the future designs of Britain."* WGW: Fk, Vol. 9, pages 400-401.

Had he done so, Sir Henry might have gained a better appreciation of the wily American general who was to deceive him not once, but twice.

General Clinton had ample opportunity to become more prudent and skeptical as he dueled with Washington. Fortunately for us, Sir Henry did not learn from his experience.

Historian John Bakeless describes a brilliant strategic deception put together by George Washington and two of his intelligence officers, Colonel Elias Boudinot and Major John Clark in October-November 1777. The object of this early deception was to prevent Howe from realizing how weak the Continental Army was while preventing the possible junction between the British forces then at Philadelphia under General Howe with those under General Clinton at New York. Had the British realized the Continental Army's weakness, they might have combined to crush it.

Washington cannily recognized a New York merchant who arrived in camp with "a dismal tale of British maltreatment" for what he was – a "dangle."[6] Washington therefore prevented his adjutant from arresting the spy and instead cleverly fashioned greatly inflated (false) strength reports from each of his (very thin) brigades. Also, by billeting his soldiers over a wide area, Washington created the impression of a force of vast size. Washington engineered an opportunity for this British merchant-spy to copy the false strength reports (the spy thus believing he had achieved an espionage coup). The man promptly fled back to the waiting arms of Sir Henry Clinton's boss, General Sir William Howe. Howe was so taken in by the supposed "intelligence coup" that when an escaped British officer prisoner brought in true figures on Washington's tiny army, that unfortunate officer was treated as an American *provocateur*![7]

---

6 A "dangle" is a term of art in intelligence work. This is a person made to appear attractive to an intelligence service while in reality under control of an opposing intelligence service. He is "dangled" as a kind of bait to lure opposing intelligence officers into becoming operationally involved.

7 Bakeless, pp. 185-187.

Not content merely to feed the British highly inflated strength figures, Washington and his merry deceivers then floated reports that Horatio Gates and thousands of American soldiers were on their way south, either to New York or Philadelphia. It was in this deception operation that Washington for the first time *"deliberately planned to use what became his favorite scheme – making sure his false information should seem to confirm itself by reaching the enemy several times from different sources."*[8]

In many ways, this early deception was a dress rehearsal for what would follow in 1780. That Sir Henry Clinton, having been duped once by Washington, allowed himself to be duped a second time in the same manner, speaks volumes about Sir Henry's credulity.

However that may be, Burgoyne's surrender confronted General Washington, far to the south, outside Philadelphia, with two problems: He had to frighten Clinton into thinking that Gates's troops, released by Burgoyne's surrender at Saratoga, would immediately attack New York. At the same time, he had to persuade Howe that those same troops would concentrate against him in Philadelphia. The sad truth was that General Gates was now foolishly keeping that army that had beaten Burgoyne idle along the Hudson, doing practically nothing, so that neither Howe nor Clinton was in any real danger.

The truth, however, was something in which General George Washington, at the moment, was not interested. If the right kind of false information could be used to delude both Clinton and Howe, the situation could be saved. Clinton would stay in New York; Howe would stay in Philadelphia; the Continental Army would be safe.

To the complicated series of elaborately arranged falsehoods required to keep the two British armies from combining forces, General Washington addressed himself with gusto, assisted by a competent group of talented and enthusiastic military liars. It was

---

8 Bakeless, p. 187.

another splendid chance for the truthful general to show his skill in forging fraudulent intelligence; and, with magnificent mendacity, he rose to the occasion. To frighten Clinton, the Continental commander-in-chief ordered not one, but three, American generals to make ostentatious preparations for an attack on New York as Clinton feared – General Philemon Dickinson in New Jersey, General Horatio Gates on the west bank of the Hudson, General Israel Putnam on the east bank in Westchester County. It was all made to look like one of those converging maneuvers in which eighteenth-century generals delighted. There was not really going to be any attack on Clinton – but Sir Henry had no way of knowing that.

> By this time, American counterintelligence had identified some local Tories who were leaking intelligence to the British in New York; but it had cannily refrained from arresting them and had let them go on sending their reports. They were useful now. Dickinson was ordered to make his preparations for an attack on Staten Island as noticeable as possible, at the same time making sure to assemble a great many small boats, the appearance of which always alarmed British intelligence officers. Gates was instructed to make similar preparations, as if to threaten Manhattan; Putnam, to threaten Long Island. After the three generals had done enough to make the supposed attack seem convincingly imminent, they were to let the secret become known to "persons who you are sure will divulge and disseminate it in New York."9

The result of this "trial run" strategic deception following Saratoga was all that Washington and his staff could have hoped

---

9 Bakeless, pp. 189-190, 193. Bakeless notes that an American spy inside General Howe's headquarters was in a position to observe the passage of the false material and the British intelligence officer's comment: *"This is a dam'd clever fellow, his intelligence from time to time has been of great use to us."*

for: instead of attacking Washington's sadly depleted force, Sir William Howe strengthened his defenses around Philadelphia and waited for 8,000 enemy soldiers who would never arrive, and Sir Henry Clinton likewise prepared for a siege of his city (from three directions) that would never take place. The two generals never joined their forces.

In the unfolding strategic deception operation in 1781 some of Washington's brightest intelligence officers, his most intrepid double agents – and not a few credulous Tories and even British agents -- played key roles. It is perhaps due to the duplicitous, but successful efforts of the "country clowns" that Sir Henry Clinton's estimates of Franco-American strength were so grossly inflated.

One American double agent, David Gray, operating in Connecticut, reported specious military strength figures to Clinton's Loyalist spy and courier, Nehemiah Marks. The credulous Marks (who had no access to the real troop strengths) unwittingly authenticated Gray's false report by reporting to Sir Henry that he faced: *"abought 6000 French troops and equal Number of Rebels and that thae expected an Reinforcement of Boston Militia & then thae ment to force Newyork."*[10]

Colonel Elias Dayton, American intelligence officer, ensured that Tory ears heard all about Washington's *"plans to have a brigade of Continentals, reinforced by militia"* stationed at Fort Lee on the Hudson – in a good location to move downstream quickly for an attack on New York.[11]

American intelligence made certain that rumors – along with bits of real information – reached known Loyalists and British spies such as Joseph Clarke and Dr. Haliburton. Thus, even enemy agents were woven into Washington's web of deception.

---

10 Bakeless, p. 333.

11 Ibid., p. 336.

Bakeless relates one story in which His Excellency, doubtless enjoying himself immensely, personally gave a boost to his own masterful plot:

> Colonel Elias Boudinot tells gleefully how General Washington managed to have a talk with an "old inhabitant of New York," well known to be spying for the British. Eagerly, the apparently naïve commander-in-chief asked questions about the water supply and landing beaches on Long Island, the terrain around Middletown, New Jersey, just west of Sandy Hook, and conditions on Sandy Hook itself. Blandly (and quite untruthfully) the general explained that there was no special reason for his questions – no, indeed, no special reason at all. He was just "fond of knowing the Situation of different parts of the Country, as in the Course of the war he might unexpectedly be called into that part of the Country." Nevertheless, he urged "the most profound Secrecy" upon the Tory.[12]

Colonel Boudinot soon heard several Loyalists – and even a known enemy agent – repeat the same claptrap that Washington had planted. Boudinot had no doubts whatsoever that Sir Henry Clinton had heard within hours all about Washington's curious inquiries.

As with the deception of 1777, there were some truthful and accurate reports coming in to British headquarters in August 1781. *But because these reports appeared at odds with the "weight of evidence," these truthful bits of information were discounted or ignored.*

> By August 18, [ed. 1781] a German Jaeger officer, Lieutenant Colonel Ludwig Johann Adolph von Wurmb, learned through spies of his own that the Americans had established depots of food and forage all the way across New Jersey. He also learned

---

12 Ibid., pp. 339-340.

that a French officer had sent his American mistress to Trenton. From these two facts, he concluded at once that Washington would march south, *but he could not convince Clinton.*[13]

In fairness to Sir Henry, the sum total of all that he observed, all that he heard, all that he read, all that he understood, pointed to an imminent attack on his island in 1781.

That said, we should also note for the record that this was not the first time that Sir Henry had been gulled by a "sound and light show" courtesy of the duplicitous General Washington. It was only the most extensive and sophisticated show that the Franco-American tricksters had yet staged. And the tricksters were playing for very high stakes.

Once again, George Washington showed his brilliance as a strategist and intelligence master. He had used his wits to baffle the British. Although the Americans lacked physical strength, they were blessed instead with canny brainpower. In the end, brainpower proved a far better weapon than firepower.

---

13 Ibid., p. 340.

# XII

# THE GREAT MAILBAG CAPER

The Hartford meeting of September 1780 was followed by two subsequent conferences between Washington and the French. Another meeting took place in Newport in March 1781 that deepened the already friendly relations between Washington and Rochambeau, but did not accomplish anything substantive since the expected second French division could not depart France due to the Royal Navy's blockade. While it is possible that Washington and his French allies may have discussed at Newport the ripening military situation in the American South – especially the strategic implications of Tarleton's defeat at Cowpens in January and British exhaustion following their unsuccessful "race to the Dan" – we lack information that such discussions took place.

What is certain is that the allied deception operation was already well underway as 1781 opened, even while Cornwallis was struggling through the North Carolina underbrush in his vain attempt to catch Greene and while Benedict Arnold was terrorizing Virginia.

What is also certain is that in far off Haiti (then known as Sainte-Domingue) Admiral de Grasse was planning his summer 1781 voyage to the American coast. De Grasse could not at that point have predicted that he would sail to Chesapeake Bay, but his letter makes clear that he understood in general terms the role his fleet would play.

On 29 March 1781 Admiral de Grasse wrote the following letter to Rochambeau (later given to Washington in translation) in which he states:

> His Majesty [Louis XVI] has entrusted me with the command of the naval force destined for the protection of his possessions in South America, and those of his allies in North America. The force, which I command, is sufficient to fulfill the offensive plans, which it is the interest of the allied powers to execute, that they may secure an honorable peace. If the men-of-war are necessary for fulfilling the projects, which you have in view, it will be useful to the service, that M. de Barras or M. Destouches be apprized of it, and *that pilots be sent to us skillful and well instructed, as the French ships have a larger draft of water than the British*. It will not be till the 15th of July, at the soonest, that I shall be on the coast of North America; but it will be necessary, by reason of the short time that I have to stay in that country (also being obliged to leave it on account of the season) that every thing necessary for the success of your projects should be in readiness, that not a moment for action may be lost.[1]

The third and final "war council" between the Allies was held 21-24 May 1781 at Wethersfield, Connecticut. The Wethersfield conference, however, was not a true "strategy session" but, in point of fact, was a key element in the already robust web of deception that Washington was spinning around Sir Henry.

Wethersfield resulted from the arrival of the French frigate *Concorde* in Boston on Monday, 7 May 1781. Rochambeau's son had arrived from France along with the new French admiral, the Comte de Barras. Perhaps of greatest importance was the arrival

---

1 Sparks, <u>Writings of George Washington</u>, Vol. VIII, p. 76. Italics added for emphasis.

of the Comte de Grasse's letter. The clear implication of the letter, combined with news that the French would send de Grasse's fleet rather than ten thousand soldiers, was that the allies would have what they had wanted since fall 1780: a powerful naval force. Time to step up the deception!

Perhaps Washington's cleverest trick – undoubtedly meant to drive home the essential points of the Grand Deception – was his dispatch of a mailbag a few days after the Wethersfield meeting containing various official documents and even a personal letter complaining about his false teeth.

Among the many letters and documents bagged by the British were "plans" for the attack on New York City – the great majority of which were generated at Wethersfield. That Sir Henry Clinton, K.B., supreme commander of His Majesty's forces in America, fell for these bogus papers "hook, line, and sinker," is clear from the fact that within days General Clinton sent copies of the materials, along with a personal note, to Lord Charles Cornwallis in Virginia and to Lord George Germain in London. Not least, Clinton had Rivington publish many of the captured papers in his *Gazette* to embarrass Washington. The strategic deception was working.

One of the key elements in the Grand Deception was its use of a mix of authentic and seemingly authentic documentation as part of the "scenery" intended to influence Sir Henry's perceptions. The Wethersfield Conference of late May 1781 provided exactly the stage required by the Franco-American deception artists. Indeed, though some real business may have taken up part of the Wethersfield agenda, upon reflection one is led to believe that the conference's chief purpose was to generate spurious documents for Sir Henry's consumption. The outpouring of such documents is impressive.

There are several aspects about Wethersfield that conventional historians seem to have overlooked or at least not taken with the proper grain of salt.

First, in sharp contrast to the highly secret proceedings of the Hartford meeting held eight months earlier, Washington seemed to want to broadcast Wethersfield to anyone who would listen. True, Hartford did produce a jointly drafted letter for King Louis XVI asking for more men and money. But its most important discussions and decisions were never written down nor revealed to the public, much less ballyhooed. The public release of the Wethersfield Circular, claiming to state Washington's military intentions, must therefore be viewed as highly suspect – especially given Washington's known habit of acting prudently and speaking with the greatest circumspection on truly vital matters.

Second, the timing of the Wethersfield Conference coincided with Lord Cornwallis's assumption of command in Petersburg, Virginia. Cornwallis's move to Virginia was known to the French-American high command shortly after it began on 24 April – a full month ahead of Wethersfield.[2] Cornwallis's destination was now clear. Moreover, his seniority to Major General Phillips ensured that Cornwallis would assume overall command of British forces operating in Tidewater Virginia. It is therefore reasonable to suppose that Washington and Rochambeau wished to draw attention as far away from their intended target, Lord Cornwallis, as was humanly possible. Making loud noises about New York in the dispatches and citing a number of reasons a southern operation was inadvisable was the perfect way to do this.

Finally, the mailbag incident – following as it did only a few days after Wethersfield – should have raised eyebrows with both Sir Henry's counterintelligence officers at the time and with gullible historians long afterward. The caper itself was brilliantly conceived.

---

[2] Idzerda, Vol. IV, pp. 88-89, states that Lafayette wrote to Washington on 8 May 1781 that Cornwallis was heading north from Wilmington to Halifax, NC, and that Phillips had returned to Petersburg, VA. While there is ambiguity about when Washington had precise intelligence on Cornwallis's destination, there can be little doubt that local partisans and Patriot cavalry shadowed Cornwallis closely and reported his movements to Greene and Lafayette immediately. As at Saratoga, when the situation required it, hard-riding couriers could cover great distances in a matter of two or three days.

The mailbag contained a treasure trove of documents and personal letters signed by the chief leaders of the Franco-American forces. Any inherently suspicious intelligence officer should have grasped at once that *the captured mail pouch gave away far too much apparently high-grade intelligence.* Why would such a group of highly experienced, combat-proven commanders as Washington, Rochambeau, Chatellux, and many others have included highly sensitive operational materials in one and the same pouch – a pouch going by regular post rider that they well knew could be subject to capture or compromise? The only possible explanation is that Washington & Company intended that the bag would be captured. And that was the idea, whole and entire.

The risk, however, is a curious one: what if a naturally skeptical and suspicious British counterintelligence officer had thought that such an "intelligence coup" was a clever plant? Such a mailbag trove was, in fact, simply "too good to be true." However, no one – either then or later – ever questioned the authenticity of the mailbag or its contents.

But the record is very clear. Sir Henry took the mailbag documents at face value, considered the collection to be genuine, and reacted strongly as his June 1781 letters to Lords Cornwallis and Germain show. He inflated American military strength far beyond Washington's actual numbers – and perhaps even beyond Washington's wildest dreams. Sir Henry, now perhaps a bit panicky, even conjured up French reinforcements and amphibious and naval capabilities that existed only on paper.

There can be little doubt that, as happened in November 1777, Clinton held the fixed opinion that New York City was Washington's target. At least, Sir Henry believed this to be true until intelligence reports came to him around 1 September 1781 that *Washington, Rochambeau and their armies were then in Philadelphia – and headed south.* Worse, he also learned about the same time that Admiral de Grasse with a powerful fleet was already waiting for the allies at anchor in Chesapeake Bay.

Of equal importance, at least from June to late August, was the distinct impression left in the minds of both British commanders that southern operations were of no interest to the French and Americans. Thus, not until early September 1781 did Sir Henry or General Cornwallis come to appreciate the true danger the latter faced as Admiral de Grasse and his fleet arrived in Chesapeake Bay rather than off New York's Sandy Hook. By then it was too late.

Washington's public issuance on 24 May of a Circular to the New England legislatures also should have raised suspicions. This is because Washington well knew that its contents would be disclosed to Clinton in a matter of days.[3] The Wethersfield Circular stated in part: *"The Enemy counting upon our want of ability, or upon our want of Energy, have, by repeated Detachments to the southward, reduced themselves in New York to a situation, which invites us to take advantage of it."*[4]

Washington was aware that four such "Detachments to the southward" had taken place between October 1780 and April 1781. These were the deployment of General Leslie to Portsmouth, Benedict Arnold sent to raid Tidewater Virginia, William Phillips to disrupt supplies intended for Greene, and then some additional reinforcements sent to Phillips immediately prior to that general's death.[5] However, Washington also knew that despite these "Detachments to the southward," Sir Henry's forces in New York

---

3 Washington was well aware that the British had their spies and sympathizers even inside legislatures, such as Dr. Benjamin Church, Harvard graduate and member of the Massachusetts assembly. Dr. Church was unmasked early in the war as a spy for General Thomas Gage. See Bakeless, op.cit., p. 9ff

4 Excerpt from the Wethersfield Circular of 24 May 1781. Jared Sparks, The Writings of George Washington, Vol. VIII, pages 51-53. WGW: Fk, Vol. 22, pages 109-111.

5 Clinton's chief interest was to establish a base in Tidewater Virginia that would be "healthful" for troops and suitable for a Royal Navy anchorage. He also intended that Phillips and Arnold cut off reinforcements and

nevertheless remained strong enough to repel any assault that the French and Americans might attempt. Perhaps Washington chose to insert this disingenuous comment partly to goad the New England legislatures into action and partly to give Sir Henry the impression that Franco-American intelligence on the strength of the British garrison at New York was grossly inaccurate.[6]

Moreover, if we accept the Circular at its face value, as some historians do, we must ask why a general as wily as George Washington would broadcast to the world his true strategic intention. Would that not have the effect of causing his British enemy to call for reinforcements and redouble his efforts at strengthening his fortifications? How could trumpeting his intentions have served allied interests if New York was the real intended target? Such a declaration would only have made an amphibious assault even more costly and risky than the allies had assessed in late 1780. Clearly, we may conclude that increasing the likelihood of failure and raising the cost in Patriot lives was not Washington's intention. Indeed, no sensible commander would make such a public announcement of his true plans and intentions.

The Mailbag Caper came about in the following way. In 1781 it was normal practice for many letters and dispatches to proceed from Washington's military headquarters, then at New Windsor, New York, to the capital at Philadelphia by regular mail – that is, by a scheduled post rider. The mail route and its schedule were well known to the Tories in the Ramapo area of New Jersey through which the post rider ordinarily would pass. This being the case, it

---

supplies from reaching Greene, thereby supporting the main army under Cornwallis.

6 As noted earlier, British headquarters in New York had been penetrated by American intelligence. The French and Americans therefore had an accurate picture of British troop strength and dispositions. Spymaster George Washington issued his "Instructions to Spies Going into New York" as a guide to what essential elements of information he desired on British plans and intentions. WGW: Fk, Vol. 20, pp. 104-5.

was not difficult for the Loyalists to lie in wait for the post rider and to hijack the mail in a manner not different from a common "highwayman" in England.

Several such thefts of mail had taken place earlier in the year. Indeed, the British had captured some of Washington's personal correspondence and published it. In one such letter to his cousin Lund Washington dated 28 March, George Washington criticized the French navy for its failure to destroy Benedict Arnold's army following the First Battle of the Capes (16 March 1781). Captured by Sir Henry and published in Rivington's *Royal Gazette* on 4 April, this letter not only embarrassed Washington personally, but created a diplomatic row with his French allies.[7] Yet, despite this serious incident – or perhaps inspired by it – Washington cannily turned embarrassment into opportunity and used the very same mailbag vulnerability to his operational advantage in late May. Historian James Thatcher, quoting from the Military Journal of 1781, noted the following:

> It has several times happened that an artful and enterprising fellow, by the name of [ed. James] Moody, employed by the British in New York, has succeeded in taking our mail from the post rider on the road, though he has had some very remarkable escapes. After the interview of General Washington and Count Rochambeau [ed. at Wethersfield], the British were particularly desirous of obtaining intelligence relative to the result. Accordingly Moody was again dispatched to effect the object. Being perfectly well acquainted with the roads and passes, he waylaid the mail for some days in the Jerseys, till

---

[7] As late as 9 May, Rivington published letters from this earlier theft, including Washington's 27 March letter to Benjamin Harrison, then Speaker of the Virginia House of Delegates, describing shortages of men and supplies. Interestingly, in this same letter, Washington refers in passing to *"the remnant of a British army"* which shows that he was not unaware of Lord Cornwallis' situation following Guilford Courthouse. WGW: Fk, Vol. 21, pages 380-383.

# THE GREAT MAILBAG CAPER 119

at length it was his good fortune to possess himself of that very mail which contained General Washington's dispatches to Congress, communicating the information which was the object of their desires. This valuable prize he had the address to bear off to New York in safety.[8]

On 4 June 1781 Moody captured the mail pouch containing Wethersfield dispatches and carried them to Sir Henry Clinton in triumph. Freeman notes that Sir Henry *"valued the seizure so highly that he gave the captor [Moody] 200 guineas but he could not refrain from boasting of his good luck and he foolishly let it be known that he was acquainted with the plans of the Americans."*[9] Jared Sparks states that *"Others [ed. letters] of a similar tenor were also intercepted, and Sir Henry Clinton seems to have considered them as written for that purpose, and designedly put in the way of being taken."*[10] Even if Sir Henry had his doubts about the authenticity of some early captured dispatches, Clinton's June 1781 letters to Cornwallis and Germain show clearly that he considered the general allied plan of attacking New York mentioned in the Wethersfield dispatches as genuine. Moreover, Clinton sent to the Ministry in London Washington's 29 May letter addressed to John Sullivan. The Ministry promptly

---

8 Thatcher, <u>Military Journal</u>, pp. 315-316. The Moody brothers, John and James, were well known Tory partisans operating in northern New Jersey and adjacent parts of New York and Pennsylvania. James was eventually to receive a permanent rank of "Ensign," a pension, and an estate at Sissibou, Nova Scotia, for his wartime service to the Crown. His brother John Moody attempted to steal Congressional papers in Philadelphia, was caught, and eventually hanged.

9 Douglas Southall Freeman, Vol V, p. 292.

10 Sparks, Vol. III, pp. 58-60, letter from Washington to John Freeman. He references the <u>Annual Register</u> for 1781, p. 123, and Andrew's <u>History of the Late War</u>, Vol. IV, p. 198. Sparks naively goes on to say: "It is certain that no such deception was intended..." Washington would have been amused.

published it in the *London Gazette* on 14 July 1781. Thus, as an unexpected (but welcome) additional benefit, Washington had the British ministry itself help spread his disinformation about the phantom Franco-American assault on Manhattan.

It is vital to view with a skeptical eye the train of events concerning the mailbag as reported by American and British sources.

First, Washington and the French generals were under no illusion whatsoever about the lack of security of the public roads and the vulnerability of post riders. Indeed, as noted, Washington had had at least two embarrassing private letters captured on precisely the same route. Thus, well aware from painful experience of the danger of losing vital documents, Washington could only be judged a fool or criminally negligent if he trusted to blind Fate that truly vital documents intended for Congress and other high officials sent by an ordinary post rider on an obviously dangerous route would arrive safely. This is especially the case if he wantonly allowed such documents to go by a post rider whose schedule was predictable and whose route was staked out by enemy raiders such as James Moody. Yet that is precisely the means Washington chose for sending his dispatches.

Second, if Washington wished to secure truly valuable correspondence from capture he could either have sent it by a personal secret courier using a route and schedule unknown to Moody and other brigands or, alternatively, Washington could have provided an armed escort of cavalry to ensure the safe delivery of the dispatches via the regular post rider. He did neither.

Third, Washington and the French commanders were hardly naïve. They surely would not commit to paper their most secret plans, tactical intentions, and weaknesses.[11] But it appears from the Wethersfield letters they did just that.

---

11 Codes and ciphers had been used even in private correspondence from before the war. Secret inks were in use by American intelligence officers and their spies by 1779.

The only conclusion that can be drawn from these considerations is that following the Wethersfield conference, Washington, with French connivance, deliberately arranged for the loss of the mailbag and its contents – some items of which were, in fact, genuine – but the key operational documents in the lost pouch were intended to mislead Sir Henry Clinton. And, as Clinton's actions showed in the days and weeks following the Mailbag Caper, the deception operation succeeded.

It should be noted that Washington had a long track record of producing bogus dispatches and orders, many in his own hand. It is perhaps instructive that in June 1781 Sir Henry fell for this trick (again) just as he had after Saratoga three and a half years earlier.

At the same time that Sir Henry was reading about George Washington's dental problems – Washington obviously had a rich sense of humor – other things were afoot, and the American supreme commander knew of them. By early June Washington was fully aware of the developing situation in the Carolinas where Nathanael Greene was steadily liberating the occupied areas and methodically forcing the British to abandon their relatively weak and scattered outposts in South Carolina.

Thanks to intelligence regularly supplied from Virginia by the observant Lafayette, Washington knew that General Phillips had died and that, as he and Rochambeau had expected, Cornwallis had assumed overall command. They also knew the approximate strength of the British army in Virginia. This was due not merely to observations sent in by Lafayette's scouts operating near British forces, but from information collected by American spies operating in Sir Henry's own headquarters.

Of greatest strategic importance, however, Washington was aware from at least early June that Admiral de Grasse and his fleet would arrive on the American coast in summer. Indeed, very quietly in late May Washington sent Allen McLane, a trusted intelligence officer and cavalryman, to Haiti to brief de Grasse on his flagship, the *Ville de Paris*. Then, in late June Washington dispatched thirty skilled pilots to aid the French fleet find its way safely into Chesapeake Bay.

And on 13 June 1781 Washington received from Rochambeau the news he had been waiting for since Hartford: that Admiral de Grasse would weigh anchor in the French West Indies in August and sail north to provide the naval power essential to destroy the British army in the South.[12]

De Grasse sent the following message to Rochambeau on 28 July 1781 advising of his impending arrival at Chesapeake Bay:

> Sir,
> I have seen with regret the distress, which prevails on the continent, and the necessity of the prompt succours (sic) you solicit. I have conferred with M. de Lillancourt, who took command of the government here on the day of my arrival, and engaged him to furnish from the garrison of St. Domingo a detachment from the regiments of the Gatinois, Agenois, and Tourraine, amounting in all to three thousand men, one hundred artillery, one hundred dragoons, ten pieces of field ordinance, and several of siege artillery and mortars. The whole will be embarked in vessels of war, from twenty-five to twenty-nine in number, which will depart from this colony on the 13th of August, and proceed directly to the Chesapeake Bay, which place seems to be indicated by yourself [ed. Rochambeau] General Washington, M. de la Luzerne, and Count de Barras,

---

12 Freeman, p. 296. Freeman states: "…on the 13th of June, confirmation came. A dispatch, highly secret, from Rochambeau, covered one in which de Grasse stated that he was bringing the French fleet to the coast of North America for a limited time about the 15th of July. Washington's mind ran ahead to what might be accomplished then." Indeed, Freeman notes a letter from Count de la Luzerne to Nathanael Greene, dated 3 April 1781, as follows: "I have now received information of the immediate dispatch of a second squadron, which is to cooperate with the forces of the thirteen States against our common enemy; it is not possible to tell the time of the arrival of the expedition at the coast of the continent, but I think it will be soon after you receive this letter." (Greene papers; Clements Library) If Greene knew, Washington knew.

as the best point of operation for accomplishing the object proposed.

I have likewise done all in my power to procure for you the sum of twelve hundred thousand livres, which you say is absolutely necessary. This colony is not in a condition to afford you such a supply; but I shall obtain it in Havana, whither a frigate will be sent for the purpose, and you may depend on receiving that amount.

As neither myself, nor the troops commanded by the Marquis de St. Simon, can remain on the continent after the 15$^{th}$ of October, I shall be greatly obliged to you if you will employ me promptly and effectually within that time, whether against the maritime or land forces of our enemy. It will not be possible for me to leave the troops with you beyond that period; first, because part of them are under the orders of the Spanish generals, and have been obtained on this promise, that they shall be returned by the time they will be wanted; and, secondly, because the other part are destined to the garrison of St. Domingo, and cannot be spared from that duty by M. de Lillancourt. The entire expedition, in regard to these troops, has been concerted only in consequence of your request, without even the previous knowledge of the ministers of France and Spain. I have thought myself authorized to assume this responsibility for the common cause; but I should not dare so far to change the plans they have adopted, as to remove so considerable a body of troops.

You clearly perceive the necessity of making the best use of the time that will remain for action. I hope the frigate which takes this letter, will have such dispatch, that every thing may be got in readiness by the time of my arrival, and that we may proceed immediately to fulfil (sic) the designs in view, the success of which I ardently desire.

I have the honor to be, &c.
Count de Grasse[13]

---

13 DeGrasse actually departed Haiti on 5 August and was well aware in early June that his destination was Chesapeake Bay, not Sandy Hook. Washington sent him thirty pilots familiar with Chesapeake and Delaware

We see further proof of Washington's true intentions – not the sham he wished Sir Henry to believe – in the following letters Washington wrote to his "adopted son."

While Lafayette was enroute to Virginia on 21 April 1781, Washington wrote:

> ...it is perhaps most probable the weight of the war [in] this campaign will be in the Southern states, and it will become my duty to go there in person where I shall have the pleasure of seeing you again. Of this I would not have you say anything. Adieu My Dr Marquis wherever you are, assure yourself of my unalterable friendship and affection.[14]

Again on 13 July Washington wrote to Lafayette that he would very soon *"communicate matters of very great importance"* by a special confidential officer and that Lafayette was to establish a "Chain of Expresses" to keep Washington constantly informed of Cornwallis' movements.[15] Why would Washington wish to keep constantly informed of Lord Cornwallis' movements if his principal concern was attacking New York City and if he had no particular interest in a "southern operation?"

That the net was shortly to close around Cornwallis also is evident in a letter Washington sent to Greene on 1 June 1781. By this time Cornwallis posed no threat whatsoever to Greene, and Washington had in all probability directed Greene to head south rather than east. Greene's forces were needed to clear the British from the South prior to the end of hostilities and the declaration of a ceasefire. Pursuit of Cornwallis was irrelevant given his move northward into Virginia and his greatly depleted strength.

---

bays in June to guide his fleet when it reached America. WGW: Sp, Vol. VIII, p. 522-523.

14 Idzerda, Vol. IV, p. 52.

15 Idzerda, Vol. IV, p. 247.

"I can only give you the outlines of our plan. The dangers to which letters are exposed make it improper to commit to paper the particulars."[16]

Washington's statement is remarkable in light of the fact that immediately following the Wethersfield conference, he and his French colleagues were *only too anxious* to commit all their "secret plans" to paper. The only reasonable explanation is that where matters of a true operational nature were concerned, Washington either used trusted couriers or remained silent, but on matters related to the deception he was only too ready to commit humbug to paper. As noted, Washington and his French associates committed all manner of "plans" to paper despite *"the dangers to which letters are exposed"* and laughed in their sleeves when Moody grabbed the mailbag on 4 June 1781. But those "secret plans" on paper were intended for General Clinton, not for General Greene.

Three letters of the many captured by James Moody and handed to Sir Henry Clinton are of special importance. The first is Washington's letter to John Sullivan, a member of Congress at the time. Perhaps somewhat tongue in cheek, Washington laments that he cannot be perfectly candid about Sullivan's operational proposal[17] *"which I dare not commit to paper, for fear of the same misfortune which has already happened to some of my letters."*

But the key element of the letter, the "bait" for Sir Henry Clinton, was as follows:

---

16 Sparks, Vol. VIII, pp. 62-63. As noted earlier, Sir Henry had written that peace negotiations would open by the end of 1781 and the territorial settlement would be decided based upon the situation on the ground. Hence, it was imperative for Washington to clear the British from as many of their southern outposts as soon as possible. Nathanael Greene was the ideal man to accomplish this vital mission. WGW: Fk, Vol. 22, pages 146-7.

17 Sullivan had proposed an invasion of Canada on 2 May 1781. WGW: Fk, Vol. 22, pp. 131-132. Washington's reply is dated 29 May 1781 from his headquarters at New Windsor.

You will have seen, before the receipt of this, by my public letter to Congress of the 27th. Instt., the result of the deliberations of the Count de Rochambeau and myself at Weathers field. That plan, upon the maturest consideration, and after combining all the present circumstances and future prospects, appeared (though precarious) far the most eligible of any we could possibly devise whilst we are inferior at Sea. The object was considered to be, of greater magnitude, and more within our reach than any other. *The weakness of the Garrison of New York, the centrical (sic) position for drawing together Men and Supplies; and the spur, which an attempt against that place, wd. give to every exertion, were among the reasons which prompted to that undertaking, and which promised the fairest prospect of success,* unless the enemy should recall a considerable part of their force from the Southward. And even in this case, the same measure which might produce disappointment in one quarter, would certainly in the event afford the greatest relief in another. While an oppertunity (sic) presents itself of striking the enemy a fatal blow I will perswade (sic) myself, the concurring exertions of Congress, of the several States immediately concerned, and of every individual in them, who is well affected to our cause, will be united in yielding every possible aid on the occasion. At this crisis, while I rejoice at the appointment of the Minister of Finance, I have sincerely to regret, that the Ministers of the other departments have not also been appointed especially a Minister of War. At the same time I am happy to learn, the mode of promotion is on the point of being finally established. With the highest Sentiments of regard etc.[18]

This letter was published in the *London Gazette* as evidence of the Franco-American "plan" to attack New York. In view of the fact that Washington was well acquainted with the impossibility of investing New York by sea and land – and also knew of the French

---

18 WGW, Fk, Vol. 22, pages 131-132. Italics added for emphasis. Deception material.

fleet's pending arrival at Chesapeake Bay – we can only judge this note as pure deception.

Sir Henry Clinton thought the intercepted letter genuine. That he did so is attested by his subsequent guidance to Lord Cornwallis and a note to Lord George Germain on 9 June. In the letter to the Secretary of State, Clinton says:

> 'I shall act offensively or defensively, as Circumstances may make necessary. But by some lately intercepted Dispatches ... your Lordship will perceive that it is not likely the Choice will be left to me for some months to come.' Clinton estimated Washington's force, combined with the French, as 20,000 fit for duty. 'My present Force is 9997 Rank and File fit for Duty.' He felt that he could not trust the New York loyalist militia and that his numbers were 'very inadequate.' However, he was 'under no Apprehensions, it be otherwise, and the Enemy command Long Island Sound, such Force might be passed over into that Island, as might make our Situation here more Critical.'[19]

It is interesting to note that, on Saturday, 9 June, Sir Henry complained to Lord Germain of having only 9,997 men fit for duty, but by Monday, 11 June, in his letter to Cornwallis Sir Henry stated his effective strength to be 10,931. Either the British army's Morning Report for Monday corrected its thousand-man error in strength reporting or Sir Henry was dissembling to Germain on Saturday. Whatever the case, it is clear that New York was defended by some 10,000 British troops – not to mention a powerful Royal Navy squadron and shore-based artillery.

A letter ostensibly to Nathanael Greene – but really for Clinton's consumption – contained the following specious humbug penned by His Excellency himself:

---

19 Sir Henry Clinton to Lord Germain, 9 June 1781; C.O. 5, 102, fols. 312, et seq., British Transcripts, in the Library of Congress.

> I have lately had an interview with Count de Rochambeau at Weathersfield. Our Affairs were very attentively considered in every point of view, and it was finally determined to make an attempt upon New York with its present Garrison in preference to a southern operation, as we had not the decided command of the Water. You will readily suppose the reasons which induced this determination, were the inevitable loss of Men from so long a march, more especially in the approaching hot season, and the difficulty, I may say impossibility of transporting the necessary Baggage, Artillery and Stores by land. I am in hopes if I am supported as I ought to be by neighboring States in this, which you know has always been their favourite operation....[20]

Yet another Washington letter, addressed to Lafayette and captured by James Moody, was handed over to General Clinton on 4 June:

> New Windsor, May 31, 1781
>
> My dear Marqs: I have just returned from Weathers field at which I expected to have met the Count de Rochambeau and Count de Barras, but the British fleet having made its appearance off Block Island, the Admiral did not think it prudent to leave Newport. Count Rochambeau was only attended by Chevr. Chattellux; Generals Knox and Duportail were with me.
> Upon a full consideration of our affairs in every point of view, an attempt upon New York with its present Garrison (which by estimation is reduced to 4500 regular Troops and about 3000 irregulars) was deemed preferable to a Southern operation as we had not the Command of the Water. The reasons which induced this determination were, the danger to be apprehended from the approaching heats, the inevitable

---

[20] Washington letter to Greene, 1 June 1781. WGW: Fk, Vol. 22, pp. 146-147. Deception.

dissipation and loss of Men by so long a March, and the difficulty of transportation; but above all, it was thought that we had a tolerable prospect of expelling the enemy or obliging them to withdraw part of their force from the Southward, which last would give the most effectual relief to those States. The French Troops are to March this way as soon as certain circumstances will admit, leaving about 200 Men at Providence with the heavy Stores and 500 Militia upon Rhode Island to secure the Works.

I am endeavouring to prevail upon the States to fill up their Battalions, for the Campaign; if they cannot do it upon better terms, and to send in ample and regular supplies of Provision. Thus you perceive it will be sometime before our plan can be ripe for execution, and that a failure on our part in Men and Supplies may defeat it; but I am in hopes that the States in this quarter will exert themselves to attain what has long been a favourite and is an important object to them.

We have rumours, but I cannot say they are well founded, that the enemy are about to quit New Yk. altogether. Should they do this we must follow them of necessity, as they can have no other view than endeavouring to sieze (sic) and secure the Southern States, if not to hold them finally, to make them the means of an advantageous Negociation (sic) of Peace.

I take it for granted that your last dispatches inform you fully of European Affairs and that you can judge from them of the probability of such an event as I have mentioned taking place. As you have no cypher by which I can write to you in safety, and my letters have been frequently intercepted of late I restrain myself from mentioning many matters I wish to communicate to you.

I shall advise you every now and then of the progress of our preparations. It would be unnecessary for you to be here at present, and I am sure you would not wish to leave your charge while you are so near an enemy, or untill you could deliver them up to General Greene or to another officer capable of exercising the command which you are in. You will always remember My dear Marquis that your return to this army depends upon your own choice, and that I am with every sentiment of esteem regd. and Affecte. Yr. etc.

P.S. My public letter contains an answer to your several favors. We have just heard from New York that Genl. Robinson is going to supply the place of Philips.[21]

A critical examination of this intercepted letter reveals Washington at his finest as a deception artist. It is simply not plausible to believe that Washington was unaware of British strength on Manhattan given the steady flow of high quality intelligence from the Culper Ring, Hercules Mulligan, Rivington and other American spies in Occupied New York. For Washington to so grossly understate British strength – giving a total of no more than 7,500 men (to *include* militia) when Sir Henry had cited at least 10,000 *exclusive* of Loyalist militia – can only be interpreted as giving the British commander the impression that American strategic intelligence was seriously flawed.

That American intelligence was *not* flawed is proved by the work of the Culper Ring and other spies, as reported by Bakeless:

> To the end of the war, the Culpers' flow of information proceeded – arrival and departure of British ships; British morale; British guesses about the peace; British losses in action; warnings against British agents in the American lines; maps and position sketches; exact location of individual units; quartermaster supplies; movements of British generals and other senior officers. Though less spectacular than some of the Culpers' other coups, it was this steady flow of accurate information that kept General Washington in touch at all times with what the enemy were doing.[22]

Moreover, so far as is known, Sir Henry Clinton had no intention whatsoever of "quitting" New York City. This can only be considered a scrap tossed in to reinforce the British view that, once again, those American country clowns had "got it wrong."

---

21 Washington letter to Lafayette, 31 May 1781. WGW: Fk, Vol. 22, pp. 143-144. Deception material.

22 Bakeless, p. 237.

But the masterstroke is to be seen in Washington's last paragraph which was intended to convey the false impression that it was allied intention to recall Lafayette to New York just as soon as it became possible for "the boy" to relinquish command of his troops in Virginia. This bit of nonsense, when added to the evolving deception, clearly was intended to allay Sir Henry's concern that Cornwallis was in any danger.

Washington had no intention whatsoever of recalling Lafayette to New York in June. Quite the contrary; Lafayette was right where Washington wanted him. Indeed, he had ordered the young Marquis on 20 February 1781 to lead a small force to counter Benedict Arnold's depredations. This mission came to an end with the failure by the French to land additional troops following the First Battle of the Capes on 16 March. Though Admiral Destouches won a tactical victory over the indolent Marriot Arbuthnot,[23] the French ships returned to Newport, thus leaving the British in control of the sea.

The arrival of Major General William Phillips in March caused Washington on 6 April to send Lafayette to Virginia once again – this time for the duration of the war. In theory, Lafayette was to report to Greene (who on 1 May 1781 gave the Marquis command of all Patriot forces in Virginia) but both generals almost certainly knew that Lafayette's real mission was to stalk Lord Cornwallis, hanging upon his heels until the British general should be run to ground and subsequently destroyed by far more powerful Franco-American forces.[24]

Adding to the growing drama was Washington's personal cameo performance. On two occasions the normally unflappable George Washington appeared to be agitated, even enraged – at least to witnesses in his headquarters. The first of these performances took

---

23 This defeat eventually resulted in the recall of Arbuthnot and his replacement by Thomas Graves.

24 See Idzerda, Vol. IV, pp. 8-9, 24-26, and 56-58, and Vol. III, Chronology, p. xxxvii.

place in May 1781 when an aide told Washington that the French wished to change his plans away from New York to some other location. A consummate actor, Washington flushed with anger and bristled at the very idea. The second boffo performance took place on 14 August 1781 when Washington paced back and forth in his headquarters, appearing to be visibly upset. From our vantage point, we can surmise that, far from being upset, the Supreme Commander was overjoyed to know that Cornwallis would soon be trapped at Yorktown between naval guns and siege artillery. We may safely assume that Sir Henry was promptly informed of both behavioral outbursts – but drew the wrong conclusions from each.

Some years after the war Rochambeau wrote in his memoirs: *"But what completely deceived the English general [Sir Henry Clinton] was a confidential letter written by the Chevalier de Chatellux ... [saying] that the siege of the island of New York had been ... determined ... and that orders had been sent on to M. de Grasse to ... force his way over the bar of Sandyhook ..."*[25]

Chevalier de Chatellux, a subordinate of Rochambeau's, only knew the cover story and probably wrote what he genuinely believed to be the objective of the Franco-American combined land and naval force. In this case, a genuine letter had fallen into British hands. But because the Chevalier was not privy to the real objective, which was to trap Cornwallis in Virginia, he unwittingly supported the growing ruse that besieging New York was the true allied intention.

Taking nothing away from Rochambeau's account, it is more probable that Sir Henry and his staff were taken in by the *totality of what they were permitted to see*, and confirmed in their assessment by failing to see what was beyond their power to observe. After all, this had happened once before back in November 1777. It is therefore hardly surprising that Sir Henry and his staff should have been duped again in June 1781.

---

25 Rochambeau, <u>Memoirs of the Marshal Count de Rochambeau</u>, Arno Press, Inc. Reprint 1971, pp. 46-47.

# XIII

# THE END OF THE SOUTHERN CAMPAIGN

The year 1781 offered new prospects to Cornwallis, but once again obstinate resistance by the colonists – both uniformed and civilian – ultimately frustrated his plans. General Nathanael Greene had replaced the impetuous Gates, and though self-taught as a military man, Greene conducted a skillful retreat and delaying action that exhausted the British forces. A true Fabian, Greene's strategy was to let time and distance defeat Cornwallis, not attempt to oppose him with brute strength.

After his humiliation at Cowpens in January, Cornwallis attempted a conventional pursuit of Greene to the Virginia state line. His thinking undoubtedly was that, if he could catch Greene, he could destroy him. And if he destroyed Greene's army the southern campaign would be won. This simplistic thinking was to lead to Cornwallis' own undoing and, ultimately, to the collapse of British rule in America.

Nathanael Greene was well aware that his militia forces and hastily trained Continentals were no match for British regulars in an open, conventional battle. Instead, he wisely used distance and time – his two great advantages – to defeat Cornwallis. This resulted in the famous "race to the Dan River" in February 1781 during which Greene steadily withdrew ahead of Cornwallis, refusing to stand

and fight, but instead causing the British commander to pursue him across many rivers and deep into the wilderness. Thanks to his troops' knowledge of the North Carolina countryside, and the military engineer services of Colonel Edward Carrington, Greene won the race to the Dan. Cornwallis's army was now exhausted and probably dispirited. We might also infer that, General Cornwallis having destroyed his baggage train in his vain attempt to catch Greene, his soldiers were hungry and in desperate need of supplies. And they were now far from sources of help along the coast. Cornwallis had no choice but to withdraw.

> The news that Cornwallis had burned his stores and was setting off in hot pursuit intrigued Greene, and he saw how to take advantage of the situation. He would begin a retreat, drawing the British farther into enemy territory and stretching their resources to the limit. He knew the routes, the fords, already had the boats lined up -- when the time was right, Greene might even be able to turn and fight Cornwallis on favorable ground.
> . . . The game of Greene, a sufficiently delicate one, was to amuse his enemy, delay his progress, beguile him with hope, onward and onward, still farther from the base of his operations, from all resources, while the country closed in upon him on all hands, and the militia, springing up from the soil, hung upon his footsteps, cutting off his supplies, and embodying for the final struggle which should give the *coup de grace* to his career.[1]

Greene followed Cornwallis' withdrawal cautiously, his only battle being that at Guilford Courthouse in March 1781. Believing that he had one last opportunity to destroy Greene, Cornwallis immediately attacked Greene's forces even though his army was

---

1 Larry G. Aaron, "The Race to the Dan," Halifax County, NC, Historical Society. See http://www.prizery.com/index.php?option=com_content&view=article&id=140%3Aretreat&catid=45&Itemid=222

depleted at this point to about 1,900 men. History records Guilford as a British victory. But although Cornwallis held the field, and Greene withdrew in good order, British losses exceeded American losses – clearly a Pyrrhic victory.

But of greater importance was the fact that Cornwallis now realized that he could not hold the Carolinas or Georgia. He had neither the military strength nor the support of the people, nor even a sham civilian government to maintain his position in the Carolinas. Hence, Cornwallis moved to Wilmington to obtain supplies and reinforcements. His plan at that point was to abandon the lower South and join with his lifelong friend, General William Phillips, who had begun a full-scale invasion of Virginia in March. Ironically, Clinton had sent Phillips to Virginia as a diversion to support Cornwallis' campaign in the Carolinas and to disrupt the flow of American supplies to Greene.

Perhaps Cornwallis had hoped to lure General Greene into following him eastward to Wilmington and then into Virginia. If so, his hopes were dashed when Greene instead headed south to clear South Carolina of the British outposts Cornwallis had established.

Whereas Cornwallis and the other British commanders in the South won nearly all their battles (the notable exceptions being King's Mountain and Cowpens) Nathanael Greene won none of his. Despite consistent losses in the conventional sense, Greene nonetheless proved the victor strategically. The British did rally a number of Tory supporters, as they had hoped, but this success was more than offset by the number of enemies they created thanks to their savage behavior toward the people. The British had to contend almost continuously with guerrilla leaders such as Thomas Sumter, the "Carolina Gamecock," "Wizard Owl" Andrew Pickens, and "Swamp Fox" Francis Marion who remained painful thorns in their "rear area." Indeed, it may be said that the British did not really have a secure "rear area" since the enraged populace and American irregular forces prevented the British from establishing any form of stable political control whatsoever. And with Greene's move south after Cornwallis' departure to Virginia, all the British victories were negated. By September 1781 the Carolinas and Georgia, with the exceptions of the cities of Savannah and Charleston, were in American hands.[2]

Later in life, reflecting upon his unfortunate American experience, Lord Cornwallis wrote ruefully: *"Greene is as dangerous as Washington. I never felt secure when encamped in his neighborhood. He is vigilant, enterprising, and full of resources."*

Morale in Cornwallis' army plummeted as it became ever clearer to the officers that they had achieved nothing and that their presence in the South not only was unwanted but was in fact counterproductive. Not only was popular support lacking for the British invasion but passive resistance by the colonists mounted as the British occupation continued.

One British officer stationed in Charleston wrote a letter to a friend in London in late May 1781 that was published months later in the *Pennsylvania Packet*. It gives a stark picture of the low state of British morale and the colonists' policy of non-cooperation:

> The retrograde progress of our arms in this country, you have seen in your newspapers, if they dare tell you the truth. This precious commodity is not to be had in the government paper which is printed here, for a fell licenser [ed. censor] hangs over the press, and will suffer nothing to pass but what is palatable; that is, in plain terms, what is false. Our victories have been dearly bought, for the rebels seem to grow stronger by every defeat, like Antaeus, of whom it was fabled, that being the son of the goddess Tellus, or the earth, every fall which he received from Hercules gave him more strength, so that the hero was forced to strangle him in his arms at last. I wish our ministry would send us a Hercules to conquer these obstinate Americans, whose aversion to the cause of Britain

---

2 "Mad" Anthony Wayne stormed Savannah in May 1782. The British evacuated Charleston on 14 December 1782. This cleared the American South of all remaining British occupation forces.

# The End of the Southern Campaign

grows stronger every day.

If you go into company with any of them occasionally, they are barely civil, and that is, as Jack Falstaff says, by compulsion. They are in general sullen, silent, and thoughtful. The King's health they dare not refuse, but they drink it in a manner as if they expected it would choke them.

The assemblies which the officers have opened, in hopes to give an air of gayety and cheerfulness to themselves and the inhabitants, are but dull and gloomy meetings; the men play at cards, indeed, to avoid talking, but the women are seldom or never to be persuaded to dance. Even in their dresses the females seem to bid us defiance; the gay toys which are imported here they despise; they wear their own homespun manufactures, and take care to have in their breasts knots, and even on their shoes something that resembles their flag of the thirteen stripes. An officer told Lord Cornwallis not long ago, that he believed if he had destroyed all the men in North America, we should have enough to do to conquer the women. I am heartily tired of this country, and wish myself at home.[3]

Even Lord Cornwallis realized that the more successful he was in the strict military sense, the farther he was from achieving the political goal of his campaign. From his refuge in Wilmington, North Carolina, after the "victory" at Guilford, Cornwallis wrote to Sir Henry Clinton the following:

Sir, I have the honour to inclose to you a duplicate of my letter of the 10th, sent by the Amphitrite, and copies of all my letters to the Secretary of State; as they contain the most exact account of every transaction of the campaign, of the present state of things in this district, of my great apprehensions from the movement of General Greene towards Camden, and my resolutions in consequence of it, I have nothing to add to it for your Excellency's satisfaction. Neither my cavalry or infantry are in readiness to move; the former are in want of

---

3 Moore, pp. 506-507.

every thing, the latter of every necessary but shoes, of which we have received an ample supply; I must however begin my march to-morrow. It is very disagreeable to me to decide upon measures so very important, and of such consequence to the general conduct of the war, without an opportunity of procuring your Excellency's directions or approbation; but the delay and difficulty of conveying letters, and the impossibility of waiting for answers, render it indispensibly necessary. My present undertaking sits heavy on my mind; I have experienced the distresses and dangers of marching some hundreds of miles, in a country chiefly hostile, without one active or useful friend; without intelligence, and without communication with any part of the country. The situation in which I leave South Carolina adds much to my anxiety; yet I am under the necessity of adopting this hazardous enterprise hastily, and with the appearance of precipitation, as I find there is no prospect of speedy reinforcement from Europe, and that the return of General Greene to North Carolina, either with or without success, would put a junction with General Phillips out of my power.[4]

Cornwallis reported to Clinton that he had 1,360 men (presumably infantry and artillery) plus 200 cavalrymen at Wilmington, but added that fully one third were sick or otherwise unfit for duty. As can be seen, Cornwallis also noted that the countryside through which he had marched was "chiefly hostile."

We have no way of knowing to what extent Washington and Rochambeau were aware of the precise state of Lord Cornwallis' troops following the battle at Guilford Courthouse. The allied commanders certainly were aware from reports sent northward by Nathanael Greene and others that Cornwallis was holed up in Wilmington with a skeletal force. It is also likely that Washington and Rochambeau reasoned that Cornwallis could not remain indefinitely in Wilmington. He would have to retire to the defenses

---

4 Debret, [p. 20] Number V. Letter of Lord Cornwallis to Sir Henry Clinton, 23 April 1781, written from Wilmington, NC.

of Charleston, sail to New York, or move north by land to link up with General Phillips in Virginia.

General Cornwallis began his overland movement northward out of Wilmington on Tuesday, 24 April 1781. His move would have been quickly spotted and reported to Washington thus removing any doubt as to Cornwallis' choice of destinations. It is therefore probable that the French and American commanders realized by May that the decisive battle of the Revolution – for which they had been waiting so patiently since October 1780 – soon would be fought in Tidewater Virginia, and most probably somewhere between Portsmouth and Petersburg.

It now became imperative for the Allies to intensify the strategic deception begun months earlier in order to prevent either Sir Henry Clinton or Lord Charles Cornwallis from suspecting the true intentions of the Franco-American commanders. In many ways, this effort mirrored that of 1777 intended to prevent Howe and Clinton from joining forces.

When Lord Cornwallis crossed into Virginia from North Carolina, the southern campaign – London's effort to detach the southern colonies – was over. Cornwallis had nothing to show for his efforts, though his fruitless campaign had cost a considerable amount of British blood, treasure, and time.

# XIV

# In Quest of Adventure

Tired and probably dispirited, General Lord Charles Cornwallis had ample time after the action at Guilford Courthouse to meditate upon the curious outcome of a campaign that had begun on such a high note on Friday, 12 May 1780, with the capture of Charleston and 5,400 American soldiers. Although his field report recording British operations at Guilford is self-congratulatory and greatly inflates both the numbers of his opponents and the extent of his "victory," it is clear this is the testimony of a beaten man.[1]

For obvious reasons, Cornwallis does not mention his use of grapeshot fired through his own lines in order to halt the near collapse of his Guards regiment.[2]

Eleven months earlier victory seemed already in hand. Any doubts about ultimate British victory had seemingly vanished after his stunning August 1780 triumph over Gates at Camden.

And yet…in late April 1781, with the frustration of the preceding four months coloring his thoughts like so many gathering dark clouds, Charles Cornwallis must certainly have been puzzled by the

---

1 Moore, pp. 479-495

2 Billias, op.cit.; p. 212

turn of events. From troop strength of 8,000 on the day of victory at Charleston, and the subsequent rallying of Tory militiamen to his standard, all he could show for his pains was a sickly, tattered force of barely 1,500 men making their way to Virginia. How could ultimate victory have slipped through his fingers?

Worse, his enemies seemed to be no weaker for his labors. They still took to the field. Indeed, his enemy Nathanael Greene was even now undoing all of his work in South Carolina. Despite prodigious feats of British arms and numerous victories in 1780, the Americans had not been defeated as he (and London) had expected only months before.

By the time Cornwallis had reached a secure base in Wilmington, he wrote that he was "tired of marching about the Country in Quest of Adventure."[3] His options were limited. *Should he garrison Wilmington and assume a defensive posture? What would be gained by this? Could he thrust back into North Carolina, retracing his steps in search of his wily opponent, Nathanael Greene? To what end? Was withdrawal by sea to the defenses of Charleston a viable course of action? Again, what would be gained? This would be clear admission of the strategic defeat of His Majesty's southern campaign. Beg to be evacuated to New York?*

Given his reduced circumstances, the only road that Cornwallis believed open to him was that to Virginia. There he could join forces with his old friend, General Phillips, and perhaps retrieve something of the disaster that, in slow motion, had befallen him in the Carolinas. Together, Generals Cornwallis and Phillips would have upwards of 6,000 men.

Sir Henry Clinton, from his perch in New York City, understood Virginia's strategic and symbolic significance. The Old Dominion, eldest of His Majesty's American colonies, was the intellectual center of the rebellion, having produced Thomas Jefferson, George Washington, and a galaxy of leading rebel figures. Virginia was

---

3 ibid., p. 213

also the most populous province and clearly a major source of provisions, munitions, and manpower. Invade and break Virginia and the American rebellion itself could be smashed.

Toward precisely that end, and to support Cornwallis, on 31 December 1780 Sir Henry sent his newly made brigadier, Benedict Arnold, to ravage Virginia. Arnold was his energetic self and moved rapidly from one county courthouse to another burning military stores and civil records and leaving smoldering ruins in his wake. County militias normally stored gunpowder and other war materials at the courthouses until requisitioned by the county lieutenant. Thus, by his raid, Arnold crippled Virginia's ability to muster local forces for self-defense. This in turn would soften up the Old Dominion for a major invasion, either overland from the south or by sea from the Atlantic and Chesapeake Bay.

That major invasion was not long in coming. Major General William Phillips arrived in March 1781 to continue the work so ably begun by his new deputy, Benedict Arnold. After further destruction of colonial supplies, the two generals set their course for south-central Virginia, evidently expecting to link up there with a triumphant Lord Charles Cornwallis marching victoriously northward from the Carolinas.

But such was not to be. Instead, in March Cornwallis was in Wilmington licking his wounds after his "victory" at Guilford Courthouse.

Making matters worse for Phillips and Arnold, Washington now sent his "adopted son," Lafayette back to Virginia to check British depredations there. This was the opening move in Washington's grand strategy planned at Hartford in late September 1780. Lafayette was only too grateful for this assignment. Not only would he be serving the man he most revered, and a cause that he regarded as his own, he would be hunting the traitor Arnold, and also settling an old family score of twenty years' standing. In 1759 General Phillips, then an artillery officer at the Battle of Minden, had killed Lafayette's father. Lafayette had a personal issue in this fight.

Rather than marching triumphantly into central Virginia, Cornwallis was now seeking to move quietly to Petersburg where he hoped to make contact with Phillips. But by May Phillips had become gravely ill and was trying to rest at Petersburg, Virginia, just south of Richmond, as Lafayette rained artillery shells on his headquarters. General Phillips, now on his deathbed, was reputed to have said: *"Won't that boy let me die in peace?"*[4] As it happened, Charles Cornwallis arrived in Petersburg just five days after his friend William Phillips died of typhoid fever on 13 May 1781.

The situation being what it was, as the senior British officer present, Cornwallis inherited Phillips' command and all British and Tory troops then in the Province of Virginia. His total force, including those in the defensive stronghold of Portsmouth, totaled about 7,000 officers and men. In a masterpiece of irony, almost one year earlier to the day, Lord Charles Cornwallis found himself in exactly the same circumstance when he had begun his expedition in Charleston. Despite all his exertions over the past year, he had gained nothing of lasting value south of the Dan River, yet he was now in command of a fresh new army of 7,000 that was ordered to chastise the Old Dominion and perhaps, just perhaps, save some small remnant of His Majesty's fast crumbling American Empire.

The Marquis de Lafayette arrived in Richmond on 29 April 1781, followed shortly afterward by Anthony Wayne and Baron von Steuben. Their presence made Cornwallis' good fortune in inheriting command of Phillips' army short-lived. Whereas his predecessors, Arnold and Phillips, had faced little real armed opposition, Charles Cornwallis' fate was to face canny and, at times, dangerous challenges from Lafayette and his associates. Worse, as summer reached its end, the slow-moving catastrophe in the Carolinas seemed to Cornwallis about to repeat itself in Virginia.

Lafayette's force was numerically inferior to that commanded by Cornwallis. Yet, like Greene, Lafayette "bobbed and weaved" and

---

[4] Lafayette was age 24 at the time. The British generals disparaged Lafayette by calling him "the boy."

could never be brought to battle on terms that would have given the advantage to Cornwallis. Indeed, "the boy's" Fabian strategy seemed to be to pester and annoy, yet stay just out of swatting range.

*What was he up to?* His presence limited the British scope for maneuver – gradually wearing down British troop strength and causing Cornwallis to use up precious supplies. But never was there to be a decisive battle. Even the so-called Battle of Blandford, a British victory over one thousand Virginia militiamen under command of Baron von Steuben and General Peter Muhlenberg, merely cost Lord Cornwallis supplies, casualties, and valuable time.

Once again, Cornwallis would grow "tired of marching about the Country in search of Adventure." Indeed, for a short time – June and July 1781 – he would march about in Tidewater Virginia, achieving little either tactically or strategically. But barely three months after assuming command in Petersburg, Cornwallis found himself in serious trouble as his enemies multiplied and his options steadily dwindled.

A little-known, but highly important mission crucial to the victory at Yorktown – and also proving that despite his "public" pronouncements Washington had his eye set on a southern operation – was his dispatch of the Philadelphian, Captain Allen McLane, to the West Indies in early June. Captain McLane,[5] a daring cavalryman and intelligence officer, had proved himself time and again as a valiant Patriot and reliable officer. Washington therefore chose him to carry a secret, highly important message personally to Admiral de Grasse.

> An intriguing mystery seems obvious here. Why would De Grasse in the West Indies, intending to attack the British

---

5 Bakeless, p. 198. McLane's work as a brilliant intelligence officer and cavalryman was well known to George Washington as early as 1777. A native of Delaware, McLane's name is variously spelled "Allan" and "Allen."

there, suddenly change all his plans? And if he were coming to the American coast, wouldn't logic dictate that he sail for Newport, where a French army and fleet were already stationed? Why would he, out of the blue as it were, decide on the Chesapeake? Obviously, it would seem that he must have been stimulated in some unexplained fashion to arrive at this all-important decision.

The answer to the riddle is to be found in the McLane papers, which reveal that the seed of decision was planted by Allan McLane, acting as special courier from Washington. This is McLane's abbreviated account of his dramatic mission: "In the interval between the appearance of Cornwallis in Virginia [ie. mid-May 1781] and the month of June, 1781, McLane embarked in the ship Congress, of Philadelphia, Capt. Geddis, as Capt. of Marines. ... Visited Cape Francois[6] in July, was examined by Count de Grasse in Council of War on board *Ville de Paris*, gave it as his decided opinion that Count de Grasse could make it easy for Genl. Washington to reduce the British in the South if he proceeded with his fleet and Army to the Chesapeake."

This secret mission which became lost in history does not rest on McLane's unsupported word. In 1820, when he was contemplating writing his memoirs, McLane obtained a corroborating affidavit from Richard O'Brien, a lieutenant on the *Congress*. In this, O'Brien says he personally commanded the ship's boat that rowed McLane to the council of war, and he adds:

"I was on the quarter deck of the *Ville de Paris* and after considerable time had elapsed one of the French officers—the Captain of a 74, one of the Council of War—informed me that, in Consequence of the dispatches delivered to the Council of War by Col. Allan McLane, his clear and explicit statements and rational views of the probable Consequences, it was then determined to abandon the Expedition against the West India Islands and to sail with all Expedition for the

---

6 Then known as "Cap Francois," and today known as "Cape Haitien," the city on Haiti's north coast was a key French military and naval base. Haiti was then known as "Sainte-Domingue."

Coast of the United States."⁷

Although Lord Cornwallis had no way of knowing it, the moment that de Grasse had received Washington's request by way of Captain McLane, his days were numbered.

On 20 June the French frigate *Concorde* departed for the French West Indies carrying thirty experienced pilots to aid Admiral de Grasse. *Of note is the fact that the pilots were specialists on Chesapeake and Delaware bays, not New York harbor.*⁸ It is therefore clear that, by late June if not a month earlier, Washington, Rochambeau, and de Grasse knew that the decisive moment was near, and the place of decision would be Virginia.

---

7 American Heritage; Fred J. Cook. Also noted in L.G. Shreve, Tench Tilghman. McLane wrote his account in the third person. His account was verified by several eye-witnesses.

8 Barnet Schechter, The Battle for New York, pp. 352-353.

# XV

# Their Lordships Confer

Eighteen months after the capitulation at Yorktown, and safely back in London, Generals Clinton and Cornwallis engaged in bitter sniping at each other as to who was responsible for the disaster. There were two central points at issue. The first point concerned Lord Cornwallis' decision to transfer the remains of his tattered force to Virginia after his humiliating "victory" at Guilford Courthouse in March 1781. Sir Henry Clinton stoutly denied that he had ever authorized Lord Cornwallis to make such a move:

> I will frankly own that I ever disapproved of an attempt to conquer Virginia before the Carolinas were absolutely restored. However, when I saw that Lord Cornwallis had forced himself upon me in that province, I left him at liberty to act there as he judged best, as may appear by my letter to his Lordship of the 29th of May, which was the first I had an opportunity of writing to him after my knowledge of his arrival at Petersburg, or of his intentions of coming there.[1]

---

[1] Sir Henry Clinton, 3 April 1783 from "Sir Henry Clinton's Observations on Earl Cornwallis's Answer," London, 1783; p. 16. http://home.golden.net/-marg/bansite/src/clintonobservations1.html.

As we have seen, Cornwallis faced a stark range of choices in April 1781 while resting at Wilmington with 1,500 sick and dispirited troops. Each of his options was unattractive.

Cornwallis's dispatch following his "victory" at the Battle of Guilford Courthouse distorted the facts of the battle to the point of intentionally misrepresenting the true state of affairs in his army and the deteriorating political situation in the Carolinas. By so doing, Cornwallis misled both Sir Henry Clinton and General Phillips into believing that the Carolinas had been "pacified," and that his army in North Carolina would soon be marching across the Dan River. Cornwallis, however, was painfully aware that the southern campaign had been lost – not merely due to his defeats at King's Mountain and Cowpens – but more significantly by the growing hostility of the American colonists and Nathanael Greene's clever move southward after Guilford.

The clarity of Cornwallis' understanding that the southern campaign had failed and that his shriveled force was best employed in Virginia is seen in his letter to his patron, Lord George Germain, in London. On 23 April 1781, one day before evacuating Wilmington, North Carolina, for Virginia, Lord Cornwallis wrote as follows to Germain from his refuge at Wilmington:

> My Lord,
>
> I yesterday received an express by a small vessel from Charles-town, informing me that a frigate was there, but not then able to get over the bar, with dispatches from Sir Henry Clinton, notifying to me that Major-general Phillips had been detached into the Chesapeak with a considerable force, with instructions to co-operate with this army, and to put himself under my orders. This express likewise brought me the disagreeable accounts that the upper posts of South Carolina were in the most imminent danger, from an alarming spirit of revolt among many of the people, and by a movement of General Greene's army.
>
> Although the expresses which I sent from Cross Creek, to inform Lord Rawdon of the necessity I was under of coming

to this place, and to warn him of the possibility of such an attempt of the enemy, had all miscarried; yet his Lordship was lucky enough to be apprized of General Greene's approach, at least six days before he could possibly reach Camden; and I am therefore still induced to hope, from my opinion of his Lordship's abilities and the precautions taken by him and Lieutenant-colonel Balfour, that we shall not be so unfortunate as to lose any considerable corps.

The distance from hence to Camden, the want of forage and subsistence on the greatest part of the road, and the difficulty of passing the Pedee when opposed by an enemy, render it utterly impossible for me to give immediate assistance; and I apprehend a possibility of the utmost hazard to this little corps without the chance of a benefit in the attempt. For, if we are so unlucky as to suffer a severe blow in South Carolina, the spirit of revolt in that province would become very general, and the numerous rebels in this province be encouraged to be more than ever active and violent. This might enable General Greene to hem me in among the Great Rivers, and by cutting off our subsistence render our arms useless; and to remain here for transports to carry us off would be a work of time, would loose our cavalry, and be otherwise as ruinous and disgraceful to Britain as most events could be. I have therefore under so many embarrassing circumstances (but *looking upon Charlestown as safe from any immediate attack of the rebels*) resolved to take advantage of General Greene's having left the back part of Virginia open, and march immediately into that province, to attempt a junction with General Phillips.

I have more readily decided upon this measure, because if General Greene fails in the object of his march, his retreat will relieve South Carolina; and my force being very insufficient for offensive operations in this province [ie. North Carolina] may be employed usefully in Virginia, in conjunction with the corps under the command of General Phillips.[2]

---

[2] Debret [pp.326-7] Dispatch Number 11; Lord Charles Cornwallis to Lord George Germain, 23 April 1781 from Wilmington, NC.

Simply put, there was nothing more to be done in the Carolinas. Cornwallis was aware, if Sir Henry Clinton was not, that the war was effectively lost in the South.

But the second point at issue between Sir Henry and Lord Cornwallis is even more significant. This concerned the matter of what Cornwallis was expected to do while in Virginia. Here the record is much less clear since it appears that Sir Henry himself held somewhat contradictory views about what should be done in the Old Dominion.

Sir Henry had dispatched Benedict Arnold to ravage the Virginia countryside – a job that Arnold did only too well between January and April 1781. Clinton billed this move as a "diversion" in support of British operations in the Carolinas. In March, Clinton then sent General Phillips with additional troops to bolster the British position in Virginia while bringing Arnold back to New York City. (Arnold would be heard from again in early September when Sir Henry turned him loose to raid Connecticut in a vain attempt to divert the French and Americans from closing in upon Cornwallis at Yorktown.)[3]

Phillips died unexpectedly in May, but the mission in Virginia was continued under the command of Lord Charles Cornwallis. In fairness to Sir Henry Clinton, this was making the best he could of a *fait accompli* by Cornwallis' presence at Petersburg. But Sir Henry did have several options. He could have ordered Cornwallis to leave Virginia and return to the Carolinas to resume the southern campaign – which was probably his preference. Clinton could have directed Cornwallis to advance up the Chesapeake perhaps with the rebel capital, Philadelphia, as his target. This had been discussed as a possible operation. Or, if Sir Henry so desired, he could have sent the Royal Navy to Portsmouth to extract General Cornwallis and

---

3 On 6 September 1781 Arnold and a raiding party of 1,700 landed at New London, Connecticut. They seized two lightly defended forts and burned 140 buildings. Clinton had sent Arnold to raid his native state in the hope that it would divert French and American attention away from Yorktown.

his whole force for service in New York or Charleston. But he did none of these things. Rather, as Sir Henry rather lamely testified: *"I left him at liberty to act there as he judged best."*

From late spring onward, Sir Henry issued a series of orders that at best were unclear and, in fairness to Lord Cornwallis, the orders often were contradictory. Complicating matters was the fact that Sir Henry's orders did not always arrive in proper sequence given the vicissitudes of delivery by fast frigate or courier. Indeed, on at least one occasion, Clinton sent one set of orders to his subordinate in Virginia only to have them arrive after Cornwallis had already received updated instructions.

What appears most probable is that Lord Cornwallis, as the inheritor of General Phillips' army in Virginia, presumed that along with that army he had inherited Phillips' mission. If that is correct, then Cornwallis's first letter to Clinton from Virginia sent on 26 May 1781 explains his planned operations:

> I shall *now* proceed to dislodge La Fayette *from Richmond*, and with my light troops to destroy any magazines or stores in the *neighbourhood*, which may have been collected either for his use or for General Greene's army. *From thence* I purpose to move to the *Neck at Williamsburg*, which is represented as healthy, and keep myself unengaged from operations which might interfere with your plan for the campaign, until I have the satisfaction of hearing from you. I hope *I shall then have an opportunity to receive better information* than has hitherto been in my power to procure relative to *a proper harbour and place of arms*. At present I am inclined to think well of York. *The objections to Portsmouth* are, *that it cannot be made strong without an army to defend it, that it is remarkably unhealthy, and can give no protection to a ship of the line.*[4]

---

4 Debret, [p. 105] Cornwallis Letter of 26 May 1781 {quoted by Sir Henry Clinton, 3 April 1783.}

It is clear from the foregoing letter, sent to Sir Henry from Byrd's Plantation, some twenty miles East of Richmond and about fifty miles Northwest of Williamsburg, that General Cornwallis had only the missions of fending off "the boy," capturing or destroying American supplies intended for Greene, and locating a suitable base for the Royal Navy. However, with the notable exception of locating a naval base, the other missions had merely been intended as supporting operations for Cornwallis' force while it was still in the Carolinas. Thus, with Cornwallis no longer in the South, the reason for General Phillips' deployment to the Chesapeake was no longer valid.

Sir Henry accused Cornwallis of departing from his plan to locate and fortify a suitable naval base without informing supreme headquarters of his whereabouts until 30 June.

> For, not having received any letter from his Lordship between the 26th of May and 30th of June, I was totally ignorant of his having changed his design, (as described in his letter of the first date) and *gone across the country towards Fredericksburg, by Hanover Court-house*; an operation which took his Lordship a complete month before he reached Williamsburg.[5]

In all likelihood, Cornwallis took the bait dangled before him by Lafayette and set out in hot pursuit of "the boy" with his superior forces. Lafayette, now reinforced by Anthony Wayne and Baron von Steuben, stayed just out of Cornwallis' reach. Like his colleague Nathanael Greene, Lafayette had no intention of letting himself be trapped and smashed by British regulars. Cornwallis did lay a clever ambush of Wayne at the Jamestown Ford, known as the Battle of Green Spring Farm, on 6 July. Although this attack was

---

5 Sir Henry Clinton's comment in letter dated 3 April 1783. "Sir Henry Clinton's Observations on Earl Cornwallis's Answer," London, 1783, p. 19. http://home.golden.net/src/clintonobservations1.html.

partially successful, Lafayette's keen eye enabled the Americans to extricate themselves. Lafayette's mission was to shadow Cornwallis' movements in and around Williamsburg and report these to Washington speedily.

The fact that Cornwallis did not move to Yorktown itself until early August and, even then, did not begin immediately and vigorously to fortify the position was critical to the outcome of the Yorktown campaign. Valuable time had been lost chasing Lafayette. Also, because Lord Cornwallis perceived no existential threat to his force, he saw no need for undue haste in raising formidable defensive earthworks. After all, the Americans in their dispatches stated that they had no interest in a southern campaign and, in any case, Washington had said that Lafayette was to be recalled to New York. Cornwallis evidently believed this.

Sir Henry does admit that, on 11 June 1781, he requested that General Cornwallis send him *"only … what troops he could spare"* for the defense of New York. After the war, Cornwallis claimed *"that the choice of a healthy [naval] station was controlled by other material considerations, particularly the imminent danger of New-York, and the important effects expected from the expedition against Philadelphia."*[6]

What is most interesting is that in his self-exculpation of April 1783, Sir Henry denied that New York was ever in danger. And yet, the record shows that General Clinton did indeed perceive a threat to his supreme headquarters – at least, Sir Henry perceived the phantom threat posed by the Franco-American tricksters with their extensive sound and light show.

In his open letter of April 1783 during his ongoing debate with Lord Charles Cornwallis, Sir Henry Clinton states the following:

> His Lordship [Cornwallis] will, however, forgive me if I cannot discover from whence those considerations arose; as

---

6 Ibid. Lord Cornwallis quoted by Sir Henry Clinton, 3 April 1783; page 24.

> my letters of the 11th and 15th of June (which were the only letters *he had then* received) do not describe New-York to *be in any sort of danger,* and his Lordship by his answer to those letters seemed of opinion, *that the project against Philadelphia was then become inexpedient.*[7]

In fairness to General Cornwallis, Sir Henry Clinton's statement that New York was not in "any sort of danger" appears either specious or highly forgetful. As we have seen, Sir Henry had indeed been duped by the Wethersfield Circular to the New England states, of which he was fully aware, and by the deceptive contents of the mailbag letters that James Moody had intercepted on 4 June 1781, not to mention Washington's brilliant "sound and light show" staged all around New York from late Spring onward.

The plain fact is that Sir Henry did indeed feel seriously threatened. On 11 June 1781 Clinton requested that Cornwallis immediately detach infantry and artillery for deployment to New York.

> ....comparing therefore the force under your Lordship, and that of the enemy [ed. Lafayette] opposed to you (and I think it clearly appears they have, for the present, no intention of sending thither reinforcement) I should have hoped you would have quite sufficient to carry on any operation in Virginia -- should that have been advisable in this advanced season.
>
> By the intercepted letters inclosed to your Lordship in my last dispatch, you will observe, that I am threatened with a siege in this post. My present effective force is only ten thousand nine hundred and thirty-one. With respect to what the enemy may collect for such an object, it is probable they may amount to at least twenty thousand; besides reinforcement to the French (which from pretty good authority, I have reason to expect) and the numerous militia of the five neighbouring provinces. Thus circumstanced, I am persuaded your Lordship

---

7 Ibid. Sir Henry Clinton, 3 April 1783; page 24.

will be of opinion, that the sooner I concentrate my force the better. Therefore, (unless your Lordship, after the receipt of my letters of the 29th of May and 8th inst. should incline to agree with me in opinion, and judge it right to adopt my ideas respecting the move to Baltimore, or the Delaware Neck, &c.) I beg leave to recommend it to you, as soon as you have finished the active operations you may be now engaged in, to take a defensive station in any healthy situation you choose (be it at Williamsburg or York town) and I would wish in that case, that after reserving to yourself such troops as you may judge necessary for an ample defensive, and desultory movements by water, for the purpose of annoying the enemy's communications, destroying magazines, &c. the following corps may be sent to me in succession, as you can spare them:

Two battalions of light infantry.
Forty-third regiment.
Seventy-sixth, or eightieth.
Two battalions of Anspach. [ed. Hessian mercenaries]
And such a proportion of artillery as can be spared, particularly men.[8]

That the strategic deception operation was unfolding as Washington and Rochambeau had intended is given more weight by the hurried exchange between the commander in New York and his subordinate in Tidewater Virginia on 15 and 30 June, respectively. Sir Henry Clinton wrote on 15 June to Cornwallis, evidently with a fair degree of concern.

My Lord,

As the Admiral has thought proper to stop the sailing of the convoy with stores, horse, accoutrements, &c. (which has been for some days ready to sail to the Chesapeak) without assigning to me any reason for so doing, I delay not a moment

---

8 Debret, [pp. 109-110.] Letter of Sir Henry Clinton to Lord Cornwallis, 11 June 1781.

to dispatch a runner to your Lordship with a duplicate of my letter of the 11th inst. which was to go by that opportunity. And as I am led to suppose from your Lordship's letter of the 26th ultimo, that you may not think it expedient to adopt the operations I had recommended in the Chesapeak, and will by this time probably have finished those you were engaged in; I request you will immediately embark a part of the troops, stated in the letter inclosed; beginning with the light infantry; and send them to me with all possible dispatch; for which purpose Captain Hudson, or officer commanding the king's ships, will, I presume, upon your Lordship's application appoint a proper convoy. I shall likewise, in proper time, solicit the admiral to send some more transports to the Chesapeak; in which your Lordship will please to send hither the remaining troops you judge can be spared from the defence of the posts you may occupy, as I do not think it adviseable to leave more troops in that unhealthy climate, at this season of the year, than what are absolutely wanted for a defensive, and desultory water excursions. [9]

In reply to his commander's urgent request, General Cornwallis wrote:

Being in the place of General Phillips, I thought myself called upon by you, to give my opinion, with all deference, on Mr. ------'s proposals, and the attempt upon Philadelphia. Having experienced much disappointment on that head, I own I would cautiously engage in measures, depending materially for their success, upon active assistance from the country. And I thought the attempt on Philadelphia would do more harm than good to the cause of Great Britain.

However, my opinion on that subject is at present of no great importance, as it appears from your Excellency's dispatches, that in the execution of those ideas, a co-operation was intended from your side; which now could not be depended upon from the uncertainty of the permancy [sic] of

---

9 Debret [p. 111.] Letter of Sir Henry Clinton to Lord Cornwallis, 15 June 1781.

our naval superiority, and your apprehensions of an intended serious attempt upon New York.[10]

Sir Henry eventually relented on the matter of recalling troops from Virginia to bolster the defenses of New York. Around 20 July 1781 he issued new orders telling Cornwallis that he might keep the forces he had, but to fortify Old Point Comfort.[11]

> I request that your Lordship will without loss of time *examine Old Point Comfort, and fortify it*. But if it should be your Lordship's opinion that Old Point Comfort *cannot be held without having possession of York*, for *in this case* Gloucester may perhaps be not so material *and that the whole* cannot be done with less than seven thousand men, you are at full liberty to detain all the troops now in Chesapeak, which I believe amount to somewhat more than that number. Which very liberal concession will, I am persuaded, convince your Lordship of the high estimation in which I hold a naval station in Chesapeak.[12]

By late July Sir Henry had convinced himself that Virginia was of little interest to Washington and that the Marquis de Lafayette was merely a military annoyance, not a serious threat. This was the second prong of the unfolding deception plan. As we have seen, the Franco-American high command was well aware that the French

---

10 Debret [pp. 112-113.] Letter of Lord Charles Cornwallis to Sir Henry Clinton, 30 June 1781.

11 Old Point Comfort is situated at the entrance to Chesapeake and is adjacent to today's Fort Monroe.

12 Letter of Sir Henry Clinton to Lord Cornwallis, ca 20 July 1781. "An Answer to that Part of the Narrative of Lieutenant-General Sir Henry Clinton, K.B., which relates to the Conduct of Lieutenant-General Earl Cornwallis, during the Campaign in North America in the Year 1781," London, 1783; pp. 167-170. http://home.golden.net/-marg/bansite/src/cornwallis0.html. This order sealed the fate of Cornwallis and his army. Cornwallis began desultory efforts to fortify Yorktown on 2 August.

West Indian fleet under Count de Grasse was preparing to weigh anchor and would be in Chesapeake Bay within a month.

# XVI

# White Flag Over Yorktown

On Thursday, 2 August 1781, Lord Cornwallis moved to the small town of York, a tobacco port on the York River, to await orders…and events. He began a leisurely effort to fortify the village – thinking that he would either move elsewhere or perhaps be evacuated by the Royal Navy. In any event, given the information he had received from Sir Henry Clinton, General Cornwallis felt himself under no immediate threat since in his view the French and Americans planned no "southern operation." Two thousand miles to the south, on Sunday the 5$^{th}$ of August, Admiral de Grasse weighed anchor and began his voyage to Chesapeake.

Sir Henry Clinton, still enjoying Manhattan, was not unmindful of his deputy in the Old Dominion. However, he suffered under not one, but *two* major delusions. The first, which had taken firm root in Sir Henry's mind certainly with the mailbag caper, if not earlier, was that the French and Americans were sharpening their knives to go after New York City. But the second delusion – perhaps less dramatic, but no less fateful for the British position in America – was that Lafayette "the boy" posed no real threat to His Majesty's forces in Virginia commanded by General Cornwallis.

That General Clinton took the bait is clearly evident from his letters to Cornwallis and his urgent requests made in June 1781 that Cornwallis speed reinforcements to New York.[1] From his headquarters on Manhattan, exactly one week after capturing the mailbag containing both official and personal correspondence in the aftermath of Wethersfield, Sir Henry stepped up defensive preparations to counter the "plans" drafted by the crafty Franco-American tricksters for their assault on his city. As noted earlier, Sir Henry now believed a *"threatened siege"* to New York by *"twenty thousand"* American troops augmented by French regulars and militia from five states to be imminent. There can be no doubt whatsoever that in mid June 1781 Sir Henry was a worried man.[2]

Indeed, Lafayette's tactical dancing game was all part of the deception. Although Arnold escaped the Marquis' grasp due to his recall to New York, and Lafayette's old family nemesis, William Phillips, was now dead, his third task was to badger Lord Cornwallis – always keeping him in sight. But keeping himself just out of reach. While it was quite true, as Sir Henry believed, that Lafayette's small force posed no existential threat to Cornwallis, the steady, but invisible flow of tactical intelligence on British movements sent by Lafayette northward to Washington certainly did pose such a threat.

But of greater strategic significance was the fact that Lafayette's small army was the nucleus around which a sizable allied force could be built at the opportune moment. And Washington and Rochambeau knew that the opportune moment was fast approaching. Each day brought the French West Indian fleet closer to Chesapeake Bay.

History records that on 14 August 1781 Washington received Admiral de Grasse's notice that he would arrive off Chesapeake – *as previously directed*. De Grasse also would bring with him the Gatinois, Agenois, and Touraine regiments, totaling some 3,000 much needed soldiers, along with 100 dragoons, 100 artillerists,

---

[1] Letter from Sir Henry Clinton to Lord Cornwallis, 8 June 1781.

[2] Excerpt from letter of Sir Henry Clinton to Lord Cornwallis, 11 June 1781.

ten field pieces, and a number of siege cannon and mortars.[3] These reinforcements would help build the critical mass needed to overwhelm Lord Cornwallis.

Rochambeau and Washington now implemented their longstanding "contingency plan." Staff preparations for the move to Virginia having been completed several weeks earlier, the French and American troops – in a high state of readiness – began moving out of their positions around New York within twenty-four hours of the admiral's notice.

Lead elements of the main allied land forces departed from their positions around New York on Sunday, 19 August, but they left behind them a "smoke and mirrors" sham that continued to mesmerize Sir Henry Clinton for another twelve days. Only about 2,000 allied soldiers under General William Heath remained around New York to maintain the fiction of a "serious threat" for as long as possible while the rest of the combined army slipped away to New Jersey and the south by 21 August.

> Pennsylvania. Yesterday, at one o'clock in the afternoon, His Excellency the Commander in Chief of the American armies, accompanied by the Generals Rochambeau and Castellux (sic), with their respective suites, arrived in Philadelphia. The general was received by the militia light horse in the suburbs, and escorted into the town. He stopped at the city tavern, and received the visits of several gentlemen; from thence he proceeded to the house of the Superintendent of Finance [ed. Robert Morris], where he now has his headquarters. About three o'clock he went up to the State House, and paid his respects to Congress. He then returned to the superintendent's, where his Excellency the President of Congress [ed. Thomas McKean], with the generals before mentioned, General Knox, General Moultrie, and several other gentlemen, had the pleasure of dining with him. After dinner, some vessels belonging to the port, and then lying in the stream, fired salutes to the different toasts that were drank. In the evening the city was

---

3 Shreve, <u>Tench Tilghman</u>, p. 147.

illuminated, and his Excellency walked through some of the principal streets, attended by a numerous concourse of people, eagerly pressing to see their beloved general. [4]

The nearly two-week delay in Sir Henry's realization that he had been duped gave the Franco-American combined forces the invaluable head start they needed to arrive unmolested in Virginia to surround the British positions at Yorktown. Washington and some advance elements reached Williamsburg on 14 September 1781 – covering a distance of more than 460 miles over muddy roads and unbridged rivers in exactly one month.[5]

The fact that the French and American forces were able to move as rapidly as they did, over the execrable roads then in existence, or by water, was made possible by considerable advance logistical planning by their staffs. Boats in sufficient number were waiting at Head of Elk to transport part of the force. This preparation did not happen by chance, nor was it done overnight. The preparations had been quietly put in place in the preceding weeks in anticipation that they would be needed. Even historians who believe that Washington suddenly decided to march south only on 14 August 1781 record that the infantry units marching overland made remarkable speed from New Jersey to Virginia.

Attention to logistics, however, is clear evidence that the Yorktown campaign was not suddenly cobbled together by the

---

4 <u>Pennsylvania Packet</u>, 1 September 1781, quoted in Moore, pp. 527-528.

5 The French had to march 690 miles. An information brochure on the Washington-Rochambeau Revolutionary Route (W3R) gives the distance from Rhode Island to New York as 230 miles and from New York to Yorktown as 460 miles; www.w3r-us.org/aa_setframes.htm. See U.S. Army Center for Military History, "March to Victory: Washington, Rochambeau, and the Yorktown Campaign of 1781," Pub. No. 70-104-1, 2007, and Robert A. Selig, Ph.D., "The Washington-Rochambeau Revolutionary Route," 2003, National Park Service, www.nps.gov/revwar/pdf/Significane%20Report-Screen.pdf.

"unexpected arrival of the French fleet" as some historians have claimed. The campaign was conceptualized and planned weeks, if not months, earlier – and was deliberately and skillfully covered from Sir Henry's view by Washington's masterful deception plan that blinded the eyes of both Clinton and Cornwallis.

Knowing Virginia to be his destination, Washington thought ahead to his need for logistical support well before the first French or American soldiers started marching overland from New York toward Yorktown. He records the following preparations – very carefully worded -- in his diary entry for Wednesday, 1 August 1781. Probably with a wry smile, Washington refers to extensive staff preparations undertaken in July, if not earlier:

> I could scarce see a ground upon wch. to continue my preparations against New York – especially as there was much reason to believe that part (at least) of the [British] Troops in Virginia were recalled to reinforce New York and therefore I turned my views more seriously (than I had before done) to an operation to the Southward and, in consequence, sent to make enquiry, indirectly, of the principal Merchants to the Eastward what number, & in what time, Transports could be provided to convey a force to the Southward if it should be found necessary to change our plan & similar application was made in a direct way to Mr. Morris (Financier) to discover what number cd. be had by the 20th. of this Month [ed. August 1781] at Philadelphia or in Chesapeak bay. At the sametime (sic) General Knox was requested to turn his thoughts to this business and make every necessary arrangement for it in his own Mind – estimating the ordnance & Stores which would be wanting [ed. required] & how many of them could be obtained without a transport of them from the North River [ie. the Hudson]. Measures were also taken to deposit the Salt provisions in such places as to be Water born.[6]

---

6 WGW: D, Vol. 3, page 405.

Having set in motion the essential preparations for the rapid overland movement of perhaps 12,000 allied soldiers, Washington's visit to Morris and Knox on 1 September 1781 while in Philadelphia undoubtedly was more than a mere courtesy call.

Washington's genius as a logistician is noted in two statements made to the President of Congress four years apart. In December 1777 he stated: *"Military arrangement, and movements in consequence, like the mechanism of a clock, will be imperfect and disordered by the want of a part."* Again, in November 1781, he noted to Thomas McKean: *"I take a particular pleasure in acknowledging that the interposing Hand of Heaven, in the various instances of our extensive Preparation for this Operation (ie. Yorktown), has been most conspicuous and remarkable."*[7] In short, preparations for the move from New York to Tidewater Virginia were hardly a hastily thrown together affair.

The French fleet arrived virtually unopposed on Thursday, 30 August, and promptly bottled up Chesapeake Bay. An attempt by Admiral Thomas Graves on 5 September to dislodge the French fleet was unsuccessful.[8] The French had gained local command of the sea.

Only in September 1781 did the scales fall from British eyes, and the respective generals finally realized their peril. General Sir Henry Clinton was perhaps the first to realize the gravity of the situation when, on 2 September 1781, he wrote to Cornwallis:

> My Lord,
> By intelligence which I have this day received, it would seem

---

7 Letters, George Washington to President of Congress, John Hancock, 23 December 1777; WGW: Fk, Vol. 10, pages 192, 197; and to Thomas McKean, 15 November 1781; WGW: Fk, Vol. 23, pp. 342-343. Along with Robert Morris, McKean undoubtedly was pivotal in making arrangements.

8 "The Second Battle of the Capes" considered by naval historians as the truly decisive battle ending British rule.

that Mr. Washington is moving an army to the southward, with an appearance of haste, and gives out that he expects the co-operation of a considerable French armament: Your Lordship, however, may be assured, that if this should be the case, I shall either endeavor to reinforce the army under your command by all the means within the compass of my power, or make every possible diversion in your favour.

Captain Stanhope, of His Majesty's ship the Pegasus, who has just arrived from the West Indies, says, that on Friday last, in lat. 38 deg. about sixty leagues from the coast, he was chased by eight ships of the line, which he took to be French, and that one of the victuallers he had under his convoy had counted upwards of forty sail more: However, as Rear-admiral Graves, after being joined by Sir Samuel Hood with fourteen coppered ships of the line, sailed from hence on the 31$^{st}$ ult. with a fleet of nineteen sail, besides some fifty-gun ships, I flatter myself you will have little to apprehend from that of the French.

I have the honour to be, &c.
H. CLINTON

P.S. Washington, it is said, was to be at Trenton this day, and means to go in vessels to Christian creek; from thence, by head of Elk, down Chesapeak, in vessels also. If that navigation is not interrupted, he should go by land from Baltimore. Your lordship can best judge what time it will require. I should suppose, at least, three weeks from Trenton. Washington has about four thousand French and two thousand rebel troops with him. H.C.[9]

It was not until 8 September 1781 that General Lord Charles Cornwallis, much too late, finally realized that his force was in mortal danger. His reply to Clinton is blunt:

---

9 Debret, [p. 193] Number VI. Letter, Sir Henry Clinton, 2 September 1781, to Lord Charles Cornwallis.

Sir,

I have made several attempts to inform your excellency, that the French West-India fleet, under Monsieur de Grasse, entered the capes the 29$^{th}$ ult. I could not exactly learn the number; they report twenty-five or twenty-six sail of the line. One of seventy-four and two of sixty-four, and one frigate, lie at the mouth of this river. On the 6$^{th}$, the seventy-four and frigate turned down with a contrary wind, and yesterday the two others followed. My report, dated last evening, from a point below, which commands a view of the capes and bay, says, that there were within the capes only seven ships, two of which were certainly ships of the line, and two frigates. Firing was said to be heard off the capes the night of the 4$^{th}$, morning and night of the 5$^{th}$, and morning of the 6$^{th}$.

The French troops landed at James town are said to be three thousand eight hundred men. Washington is said to be shortly expected; and his troops are intended to be brought by water from the head of Elk, under protection of the French ships. The Marquis de la Fayette is at or near Williamsburgh: The French troops are expected there, but were not arrived last night. As my works were not in a state of defence, I have taken a strong position out of the town. I am now working hard at the redoubts of the place. Provisions for six weeks: I will be very careful of it.

I have the honour to be, &c.
CORNWALLIS[10]

It is highly likely that both British generals now realized they had been royally duped. The Grand Deception had kept General Cornwallis blissfully unaware until September that he would be surrounded and destroyed before he could complete his fortifications. At the same time, Washington's "sound and light show" diverted Sir Henry's attention away from the allies' real objective – destruction of the British expeditionary force in

---

10 Debret, Number V. Letter of Lord Charles Cornwallis, 8 September 1781, to Sir Henry Clinton.

Virginia. It was now too late for Sir Henry either to reinforce or extract Cornwallis and his army. Clinton, too, had been blinded by Washington's Grand Deception.

Lafayette already being in place, the arriving French and American units quickly threw a cordon around the stunned British. The American army began concentrating in force around York on 26 September and formal siege operations were begun on 6 October. Five days later the French and Americans constructed a "parallel" that was within 200 yards of Cornwallis' positions. With allied siege artillery in place, and no hope of relief by sea, Lord Charles Cornwallis now found himself in precisely the same unenviable situation that he, Cornwallis, had placed the unfortunate Benjamin Lincoln at Charleston in May 1780.

> When the French fleet arrived, Cornwallis and his army were doomed. General Thomas Nelson was present [ed. Yorktown was his home] leading the Virginia Militia. Here was born one of the most famous legends of the Revolution. Nelson is alleged to have given the order for the artillery to fire on his own house, which, it was presumed, was occupied by Cornwallis himself. He is even alleged to have offered 5 guineas to the first man to hit the house. Whether this actually happened or not is open to speculation as there is no documented evidence to support the claim. However, the Nelson House was the largest, nicest house in Yorktown – fitting quarters for a British Lord. It is also a fact that the interior of the Nelson House was destroyed by cannon fire and that cannon balls are still lodged within its walls.[11]

---

11 Unpublished paper written for Fairfax Resolves chapter of SAR by W. Page Johnson II, a direct descendent of Thomas Nelson. On 11 June 1781, Nelson succeeded Thomas Jefferson as governor of Virginia. As a member of the House of Burgesses for York County, Nelson had been instrumental in the formation of the Virginia militia and, in July 1775, had been appointed colonel of the 2nd Virginia Infantry Regiment. Paper is in possession of the authors. See also http://www.nps.gov/york/historyculture/nelson-house.htm.

Five months almost to the day of his assumption of command in May, Lord Cornwallis took his place in American history as his drummer beat a parley and the British commander raised the white flag of surrender at the small Virginia town of York. The surrender ceremony took place on Friday, 19 October 1781. The British commanders in America had at last not only been thoroughly puzzled by George Washington's massive common sense and great imagination, but outgeneraled and decisively beaten.

Lord Cornwallis' American adventure was finally over.

America's adventure was about to begin.

# XVII

# Epilogue

Yorktown was not quite the end. During 1782 several more land battles took place in the territory that was about to be formally recognized as the United States of America, especially in the South and the Ohio Valley. Raiders like Simon Girty continued to threaten settlers in Kentucky and Ohio. Moreover, throughout 1782 the British still occupied a few cities on the Atlantic seaboard, notably Charleston and New York, and a number of forts in the Great Lakes area. George Washington sternly insisted that the war had not ended and continued to recruit and train his Continental Army for another eighteen months against the possibility of a resumption of major hostilities.

But, for all intents and purposes, the British had by the end of 1781 finally concluded that the costly American war should be ended. Yorktown sent shock waves through the political establishment in London. All the colonies – north and south together – were irretrievably lost. And the sooner that a reasonable peace could be concluded, the better it would be for British interests not only in North America, but elsewhere in the world.

The Yorktown defeat provoked a series of "No Confidence" votes in the House of Commons that finally forced Lord North's resignation as Prime Minister on 20 March 1782.[1] Lord Rockingham replaced Lord North and gave instructions to negotiate the independence of the United States. However, Rockingham died unexpectedly in July and his political ally, Lord Shelburne, thereupon became Prime Minister. Shelburne was equally anxious to grant a generous peace settlement because he believed that the former British colonies, now States, presented lucrative trade opportunities to Great Britain.

In May 1782 Sir Henry Clinton was called home after nearly seven years' service in America. His replacement, Sir Guy Carleton, maintained an "armed truce" from his post in New York City until instructed by Parliament in 1783 to prepare to evacuate British forces and Loyalists from America. Sir Guy completed this move on 25 November 1783 and for nearly a century afterward that day was commemorated as Evacuation Day. All remaining British forces and some 20,000 Loyalists sailed from New York. This former holiday was only replaced in 1863 when Abraham Lincoln proclaimed the last Thursday in November to be a national day of Thanksgiving.

British Admiral Sir George Rodney did win a spectacular victory over Comte de Grasse at the Battle of the Saintes in April 1782. This naval victory in the West Indies somewhat bolstered the shaky British negotiating position as the diplomats began their work that year in Paris. At Rockingham's direction – quite apart from talks with Vergennes – the British quietly opened peace talks with their American opposite numbers in Paris.

In February 1783 George III issued his Proclamation of Cessation of Hostilities – a clear signal that a peace treaty was not far off. American peace commissioners in France – Benjamin Franklin, John Adams, and John Jay – reviewed the proposals put before them by Lord Shelburne's representative, Richard Osborne.

---

1 Tuchman, op.cit., p. 227, notes the following: "When Lord North, still held in office by the King, asked Parliament for a further large war loan, the House finally balked, the Government's majority broke and the King in his misery drafted, though he did not deliver, a message of abdication."

# EPILOUGE

After some seventeen months of talks, with considerable wrangling over commercial rights, the final Peace of Paris was signed on 3 September 1783 thus formally ending the American War of Independence.

But even the Peace of Paris of 1783 did not really end the war for some.

Years of controversy dogged several of the senior British commanders, notably Sir Henry Clinton, Lord Charles Cornwallis, Admiral Lord Richard and General Sir William Howe, and "Gentleman Johnny" Burgoyne. Bitterness and recrimination continued until death carried these men away. The British ministries that negotiated with the Americans faced growing antipathy from elements in commercial and nationalist groups over the peace treaty's provisions. In effect, for many years Great Britain experienced what might have been called a "Who Lost America" debate.

In America, attention turned toward building a new republican political structure that in 1787 resulted in the "Miracle at Philadelphia" – the United States Constitution. Victory at Yorktown and the Peace of Paris also opened to settlement the rich territories of the Ohio Valley and beyond. A new country had been born and with it, a sense of destiny and optimism. The American idea would spread over a continent in the following century. Suspicion of Great Britain – and conflict – would remain an element of American attitudes, actions, and politics until well after the Civil War.

Fortunately, with the passage of time old wounds heal and new relationships grow. It is good that this is so. But at the same time, we should be mindful that the precious legacy we have received is ours due to the vision and steadfast courage of George Washington and those who stood by him. We would do well to remember that Washington not only was a man of *"massive common sense and reasoning power"* but also possessed that indispensable *"element of legerdemain"* that marks a truly great commander. He left his enemies not only beaten, but completely puzzled.

Fittingly, it is George Washington who should have the last word on the Revolution he had just won. In a somewhat philosophic mood, Washington wrote to his deputy and friend, Nathanael Greene, reflecting on their eight years of struggle:

> If Historiographers should be hardy enough to fill the page of History with the advantages that have been gained with unequal numbers, on the part of America, in the course of this contest, and attempt to relate the distressing circumstances under which they have been obtained, it is more than probable that Posterity will bestow on their labors the epithet and marks of fiction; for it will not be believed that such a force as Great Britain has employed for eight years in this Country could be baffled in their plan of Subjugating it by numbers infinitely less, composed of Men oftentimes half starved; always in Rags, without pay, and experiencing, at times, every species of distress which human nature is capable of undergoing.[2]

Perhaps Washington's dream of independence for America became reality because, as he had hoped, the finger of Providence – with a little help from some imaginative Earthly "country clowns" – had succeeded in blinding the eyes of his enemies.

### *Ars est celare artem*

> The Continental troops that remain with us are as good as the enemy in every respect, and they have a fortitude in their misery that is unknown to European armies.
>
> Lafayette
> Letter to Comte de Vergennes

---

2 WGW: Fk, Vol. 26, pp. 103-4. George Washington letter to Nathanael Greene, 6 February 1783.

# BIBLIOGRAPHY

**PUBLICATIONS AND PAPERS**

Adams, John. <u>The Works of John Adams, Second President of the United States: with a Life of the Author, Notes and Illustrations, by his Grandson Charles Francis Adams.</u> Boston: Little, Brown and Co., 1856. 10 volumes. Vol. 10. Chapter: *TO H. NILES*.

Aaron, Larry G., "The Race to the Dan," Halifax County (NC) Historical Society; South Boston, Virginia, 1999

Bakeless, John, <u>Turncoats, Traitors & Heroes: Espionage in the American Revolution</u>; J. B. Lippincott, 1959; republished by DaCapo Press, New York, 1998

Billias, George Athan, <u>George Washington's Generals and Opponents</u>, William Morrow, New York, 1964, republished by DaCapo Press, 1994.

Brown, Anthony Cave, <u>Bodyguard of Lies</u>, Harper and Row, New York, 1975

Charlton, James, ed. <u>The Military Quotation Book;</u> Thomas Dunne Books, St. Martin's Press, New York, 2002.

Chernow, Ron, <u>George Washington, A Life</u>, The Penguin Press, New York, 2010

Clausewitz, Carl von. <u>On War.</u> Ed. and trans. Michael Howard and Paret, Peter.

Princeton, NJ: Princeton University Press, 1976.

Cook, Fred J., American Heritage; Vol. VII, No. 6; October 1956

Davis, Burke, The Campaign that Won America, The Story of Yorktown, Eastern Acorn Press, Philadelphia,1979

Dupuy, Ernest and Trevor N. Dupuy, The Encyclopedia of Military History from 3500 B.C. to the Present, Harper and Row, New York,1970

Ellis, Joseph J., His Excellency George Washington; Alfred A. Knopf, New York, 2004

Fitzpatrick, John C., ed.; The Writings of George Washington from the Original Manuscript Sources: 1745-1799, [WGW: Fk] Vol. 22; April 27, 1781 – August 15, 1781 United States Government Printing Office

Fortescue, Sir John; The War of Independence, The British Army in North America, 1775-1783; Macmillan and Co., London, 1911; republished by Stackpole Books, Mechanicsburg, Pennsylvania, 2001

Freeman, Douglas Southall; George Washington: A Biography, seven volumes; completed by J.A. Carroll and M.W. Ashworth, New York, 1948-1957

Hayek, Friedrich von; The Counterevolution of Science: Studies on the Abuse of Reason; Liberty Press, Indianapolis, 1979.

Hibbert, Christopher, Redcoats and Rebels; W. W. Norton & Company, New York, 1990

Hills, John. Surveyor. A chart of the bar of Sandy Hook the entrance of Hudson's River in the Province of New Jersey; survey'd in 1782 by Lieutt. Hills, of the 23d Regt. And private draftsman to His Excellency the Commander in Chief (London: Wm. Faden) 1784. Accessed August 28, 2010. http://lcweb2.loc.gov/cgi-bin/map-item.pl

Hofstadter, Richard; William Miller, and Daniel Aaron; The United States: The History of a Republic; Prentice-Hall, Englewood Cliffs, NJ; 1957

Hughes, Rupert, The Savior of the States, 1777-1781; William Morrow and Co., New York, 1930

Idzerda, Stanley J., et al, eds., Lafayette in the Age of the American Revolution: Selected Papers and Letters, 1776-1790; Cornell University Press, Ithaca, NY 1977

Jackson, Donald, ed. and Dorothy Twohig, The Papers of George Washington, University of Virginia Press, Charlottesville, VA; 1978

Jensen, Merrill, The Founding of a Nation: A History of the American Revolution 1763-1776; Oxford University Press, 1968

Johnson, W. P. II, "Thomas Nelson, Jr. 1738-1789," unpublished paper presented 14 April 2011 to the Fairfax Resolves Chapter, Sons of the American Revolution

Kennedy, David M., Lizbeth Cohen, Thomas A. Bailey, The American Pageant, Wadsworth, Boston, 200

Lamborn, G.L. The People in Arms, Small Wars Journal (electronic) and Defense Intelligence Agency (paper), 2009

Mahan, Alfred Thayer, The Influence of SeaPower upon History: 1660-1815; Prentice-Hall, Englewood Cliffs, NJ; 1980

Moore, Frank, Diary of the Revolution 1775-1781, Washington Square Press, Inc., New York, 1968

Montrésor, John, A plan of the city of New-York & its environs to Greenwich, on the North or Hudsons River, and to Crown Point, on the East or Sound River, shewing the several streets, publick buildings, docks, fort & battery, with the true form & course of the commanding grounds, with and without the town. Survey'd in the winter, 1766. P. Andrews, sculp. London 1766. Library of Congress Map Collection http://memory.loc.gov/cgi-bin/map_item.pl (accessed 12 June 2011)

"National Park Service Maps" Accessed 28 Aug 2011 www.nps.gov/carto/PDF/AMREAmap7.pdf.

Rochambeau, Comte de, <u>Memoirs of the Marshal Count de Rochambeau</u>, Arno Press, Inc.; New York, reprinted 1971

Schutz, John A. and Douglass Adair, eds., <u>The Spur of Fame: Dialogues of John Adams and Benjamin Rush, 1805-1813</u>; Huntington Library; San Marino, CA; 1966

Schecter, Barnet, <u>The Battle for New York</u>, Walker and Company, New York, 2002

Schecter, Barnet, <u>George Washington's America, a biography through his maps,</u> Walker and Company, New York, 2010

Shreve, L.G., <u>Tench Tilghman: The Life and Times of Washington's Aide-de-Camp</u>; Tidewater Publishers, Centreville, Maryland, 1982

Simons, Daniel J. and Christopher F. Chabris, "Gorillas in our midst: sustained inattentional blindness for dynamic events," <u>Perception</u>, Vol. 28; Harvard University Press, 1999

Sparks, Jerad, ed.; <u>Writings of George Washington</u>, John B. Russell, Boston, 1837

Sun Tzu. <u>The Art of War.</u> Trans. Samuel B. Griffith, New York: Oxford University Press, 1963.

Thacher, James, M.D.; <u>Military Journal During the American Revolutionary War from 1776 to 1783</u>, published 1823

Tuchman, Barbara, <u>The March of Folly From Troy to Vietnam</u>, Alfred A. Knopf, New York, 1984

Twohig, Dorothy, ed.; <u>The Diaries of George Washington</u>, University of Virginia Press, Charlottesville, VA, 1979

Weigley, Russell F., <u>Eisenhower's Lieutenants</u>, Indiana University Press, Bloomington, Indiana, 1981

## INTERNET SOURCES

Curtis, Edward E, Ph. D. *AMERICAN REVOLUTION.ORG* "The organization of the British Army in the American Revolution" New Haven, Yale University Press, London Oxford University Press, 1976. http://americanrevolution.org/archives.html. Accessed March 1, 2011

Buried History of the American Revolution, *The British Army in America 1776 to 1781* www.redcoat.me.uk/armylists.htm Accessed April 11, 2011

Washington – Rochambeau Revolutionary Route, *Our Main Brochure* dated July 14 2009 www.w3r-us.org/aa_setframes.htm. Accessed May 31, 2011

Haley, John Williams, *Washington's Third Visit to Rhode Island* www.quahog.org/factsfolklore/index.php?id=156 (last edited February 20, 2007)

American History to 1865, "A Colonist Reports on the Debate in Parliament on the Stamp Act (Isaac Barre's speech)" http://www.pasleybrothers.com/mocourses/texts/Barre.htm (accessed August 2011)

Answers.com "Revolutionary War" "Costs of the War" "Financial Costs: http://www.answers.com/topic/american-revolutionary-war#costs_of_the_war (

*Oatmeal for Fox Hounds* "Source Documents Index" "Cornwallis, Charles Earl, 'An Answer To That Part Of The Narrative Of Lieutenant-General Sir Henry Clinton, K.B. Which Relates To The Conduct Of Lieutenant-General Earl Cornwallis'. February 1783" http://home.golden.net/marg/bansite/src/cornwallis0.html (accessed March 17, 2011)

*Oatmeal for Fox Hounds* "Source Documents Index" "Clinton, Sir Henry K.B. 'The Narrative Of Lieutenant-general Sir Henry Clinton', January 1783" http://home.golden.net/~marg/bansite/src/clintonnarrative.html (accessed March 17, 2011)

*Oatmeal for Fox Hounds* "Source Documents Index" "Clinton, Sir Henry K.B.. 'Sir Henry Clinton's Observations on Earl Cornwallis's Answer'. April 1783" http://home.golden.net/marg/bansite/src/clintonobservations1.html (accessed March 17, 2011)

"George Germain, 1st Viscount Sackville." *Wikipedia, The Free Encyclopedia*. Wikimedia Foundation, Inc. 2004. 5 September 2011. <http://www.enotes.com/topic/George_Germain,_1st_Viscount_Sackville>

National Park Service. *The Washington-Rochambeau Revolutionary Route, Statement of National Significance Revised Draft Report January 30, 2003*. http://www.nps.gov/revwar/pdf/Significance Report-Screen.pdf

National Park Service "Yorktown Battlefield" *The Nelson House* www.nps.gov/york/historyculture/nelson-house.htm Accessed 2011

# The Americans

### Nathanael Greene (1742-1786)

Nathanael Greene was born into a Quaker family in Potowomut, Rhode Island, in Warwick Township on 7 August 1742, and – despite Quaker discouragement of academic learning – educated himself in law and mathematics. In all probability Greene would have become a teacher, as he was greatly influenced by Rev. Ezra Styles, president of Yale College. In 1770 Greene had advocated the establishment of a public school in Coventry, Rhode Island, and was elected to the provincial legislature as a Whig in 1771 and for several years thereafter.

The growing crisis in the colonies caused him to enlist as a private in the Rhode Island militia in 1774 and to begin teaching himself the elements of military strategy. Greene especially studied the campaigns of the French general Turenne under Louis XIV. His military involvement caused Greene to be expelled from the Society of Friends.

Upon the outbreak of hostilities in 1775, Greene was elected commander of the Rhode Island troops and joined the American forces at Cambridge, Massachusetts. Congress appointed Greene as a brigadier general in June 1775. Washington named Greene to command Continental troops in Boston after its evacuation by Howe in March 1776. From that date until the end of the Revolution George Washington considered the self-taught Nathanael Greene to be one of his most trusted and competent generals. Greene commanded troops at Trenton, Brandywine, Germantown, and Monmouth. From 1778 to 1780 Greene served as Quartermaster General and handled the position well despite meager resources and little help either from Congress or the state legislatures.

In October 1780 Washington appointed Greene commander of the Southern army and instructed him to clear the Carolinas of the scattered British outposts there. His tactical masterpiece is perhaps the "Race to the Dan" in which he exhausted and frustrated his British opponent, Lord Charles Cornwallis. Although General Greene did not win a single battle, of greater importance is the fact that his strategy caused British occupation of the American South to collapse. The Carolinas and Georgia were cleared of British forces prior to the cessation of hostilities. Nathanael Greene died at his plantation at Mulberry Grove, Georgia, on 19 June 1786. His epitaph might well be his comment: *"We fight, get beat, rise, and fight again."*

### Allen McLane (1746-1829)

Allen McLane was born in Philadelphia sometime in 1746 and became a cavalry officer during the American Revolution. He soon became involved in intelligence operations where he proved himself adept and reliable.

Captain McLane served at the Battles of Great Bridge and Long Island, the defense of New York, White Plains, the Trenton-Princeton campaign, and Brandywine. Following Brandywine, McLane was detached for the purpose of raising a contingent from Delaware. It is believed that McLane used his personal fortune to equip and pay the soldiers of his regiment.

Returning to the main army in December 1777, George Washington directed McLane and his cavalry to screen the Continental Army as it moved into winter quarters at Valley Forge following the evacuation of Philadelphia. McLane is credited with detecting British forays out of Philadelphia and giving timely warning to American commanders thereby enabling them to take precautionary measures and avoid ambush.

After Valley Forge, McLane served at Monmouth, Stoney Point, and Paulus Hook. Early in 1780 Washington sent McLane to reinforce General Benjamin Lincoln at Charleston. Narrowly escaping capture, McLane then served under Baron von Steuben. McLane was promoted to Major in 1780.

McLane's most important mission was his voyage in the *Congress* to Cap Francais in Sainte Domingue (today's Haiti) bearing messages from Washington and Rochambeau for Admiral de Grasse. This exceptional mission helped pave the way for Yorktown.

Major McLane left the army on 31 December 1781. He had given away his personal fortune, but went into partnership with Robert Morris. The State of Delaware appointed McLane a "marshal" and he became a public official in that state. During the War of 1812, Allen McLane commanded the defenses of Wilmington, Delaware.

McLane died in Wilmington at the age of 83 on 22 May 1829.

### Tench Tilghman (1744-1786)

Tench Tilghman was born 25 December 1744 in Talbot County, Maryland, on his father's plantation "Fausly." His father, James Tilghman, was a prosperous lawyer who moved to Philadelphia where he served as secretary to the Pennsylvania Proprietary Land Office among other positions of trust. James and his wife had 12 children, to include six sons, of whom Tench was the eldest. All six sons received good educations and distinguished themselves in their respective fields.

When hostilities with Great Britain loomed in 1775, Tench Tilghman joined a light infantry unit from Philadelphia called the "Silk Stockings." He served as a lieutenant in this unit, though in the summer he was promoted to captain and was made secretary of a commission headed by Major General Philip Schuyler whose mission was to secure the neutrality of the Iroquois Confederation in western Pennsylvania. The commission was successful in negotiating a treaty of peace with the Indians.

When the "Silk Stockings" became part of Washington's army early in 1776, Tench Tilghman was selected to become a member of Washington's staff due to his education and family ties. Intelligent and industrious, Tilghman soon became one of Washington's most trusted aides. Colonel Tilghman accompanied his chief in all his major actions, and served as well as aide-de-camp to the Marquis de Lafayette.

When Lord Cornwallis surrendered at Yorktown, George Washington appointed his faithful aide, Tench Tilghman, to carry the happy news personally to Congress, then meeting in Philadelphia. It is said that Tilghman rode his horse to the very steps of the building then housing Congress with the articles of surrender in his hand.

After the Revolution, Tench Tilghman returned to Philadelphia and formed "Tench Tilghman and Company" in partnership with Robert Morris. Unfortunately, Tilghman contracted hepatitis and died on 18 April 1786.

George Washington, writing to James Tilghman from Mount Vernon, stated: *"I may venture to assert (that excepting those of his nearest relatives) none could have felt his death with more regret than I did because no one entertained a higher opinion of his worth, or had imbibed sentiments of greater friendship for him than I had done."*

# The British

### Sir Henry Clinton (1730-1795)

Lieutenant General Sir Henry Clinton was born about 16 April 1730, the son of Admiral George Clinton, royal governor of the Province of New York.  His family could trace its lineage to the Norman Conquest of 1066, and his family had a long and distinguished history of service to the English Crown.  At age 15, Henry Clinton joined the New York militia and served as a lieutenant during King George's War (1740-1748).  He was given garrison duty at the captured fortress of Louisbourg.  Clinton went to London in 1749 and was commissioned a captain in the British army in 1751.  He served in Europe as a lieutenant colonel during the Seven Years War (1756-1763) and was seriously wounded at the Battle of Freiberg.  Clinton became aide-de-camp to Duke Ferdinand of Brunswick, with whom he established a lifelong friendship.

During the Seven Years War, Clinton formed a number of friendships and acquaintances that he would meet again during the American Revolution.  He became a close friend of William Phillips who would die in Virginia, and an acquaintance of Charles Cornwallis, both of whom would become British generals.

Another pair of friends from his days in Germany were William Alexander [later, Lord Stirling] and Charles Lee, who would join the American rebels as generals and oppose him on the battlefield.

Promoted to Major General in 1772, Clinton was sent to Massachusetts in 1775 where he served first under General Thomas Gage and later under General Sir William Howe. He fought with distinction at Bunker Hill and was the staff officer who drew plans for the conquest of Long Island in September 1776 for which he was knighted. Upon General Howe's resignation in 1778, Sir Henry Clinton became commander-in-chief due largely because no other senior British officer was available or would accept the position.

General Clinton carried out orders from Lord Germain to invade the southern colonies in early 1780 and personally commanded British forces at Charleston, South Carolina, in May 1780. Returning to New York, Clinton left Cornwallis to carry out operations in the American South, often providing little clear guidance to Cornwallis. In May 1782 Sir Henry returned to Great Britain to find that Cornwallis was viewed with sympathy and he, Clinton, was held to blame for the disaster at Yorktown. This triggered a bitter – and highly public – duel of words between Clinton and Cornwallis for a number of years. Sir Henry Clinton died in Cornwall on 23 December 1795 before he could take up his duties as Governor of Gibraltar. Two of his sons later became British generals.

### Lord Charles Cornwallis (1738-1805)

Charles Cornwallis, 1st Marquess and 2nd Earl Cornwallis, was born in London on 31 December 1738 and was destined for a career as a soldier. Educated at Eton and Clare College, Cambridge, Cornwallis served in Europe during the Seven Years War (1756-1763) during which time he inherited his father's titles and estate. He served at the Battle of Minden in 1759 ending the war as a lieutenant colonel. In 1762 Cornwallis entered the House of Lords and, politically well-connected, became aide-de-camp to King George III in 1765 and governor of the Tower of London five years later.

Politically a Whig, and an ally of Rockingham, Cornwallis was personally opposed to the coercive measures enacted by Parliament that had angered the American colonists, but as a professional soldier felt duty bound to fight against the Americans on behalf of his king. Lord Cornwallis chased the remnants of the American forces across New Jersey after their defeat in New York in September 1776. However, at year's end Cornwallis was outmaneuvered at Trenton and Princeton by Washington and forced to withdraw.

Considered one of the most skilled British generals, Lord Cornwallis was placed in command of the expeditionary forces sent to subdue the American South in 1780. Although initially successful, Cornwallis experienced reverses at King's Mountain and Cowpens, and witnessed the "withering away" of his forces in the Carolinas. Moving into Virginia he was eventually trapped at Yorktown and compelled to surrender on 19 October 1781, thus effectively ending the war in America.

Lord Cornwallis went on to a distinguished career as governor general of India from 1786 to 1791 and as viceroy of Ireland from 1798 to 1801 where his personal and political skills won the goodwill of both the Irish and the Orangemen, foiled a French invasion, and paved the way for the Act of Union. In 1801 Cornwallis was named Britain's chief negotiator with France; his diplomacy helped bring about the Treaty of Amiens with Napoleon. Appointed a second time to be governor general of India, Lord Cornwallis died in that country on 5 October 1805.

### George Sackville (1716-1785)

George Sackville, better known as Lord George Germain, was born in London on 26 January 1716, the third son of Lionel

Cranfield Sackville, 1st Duke of Dorset. He was educated at Westminster and Trinity College, Dublin, and held the titles 1st Viscount Sackville of Drayton and Baron Bolebrooke of Sussex. Germain began his career as a soldier, being appointed Captain in 1737, but rose rapidly to the rank of Major General in 1755 and to Lieutenant General in 1757 during the Seven Years War.

As Lieutenant General, Sackville had been in command of five regiments of British cavalry at the pivotal Battle of Minden, Germany, on 1 August 1759. As the sanguinary battle between the Prussians and French drew to a close, Duke Ferdinand of Brunswick, Allied commander, realized that victory was within his grasp. He ordered Sackville to attack the disorganized French. Sackville sullenly refused to move. Sackville refused not once, but three times. As a result, the French army, although beaten, was able to withdraw unhindered to the Rhine. Sackville was subsequently court-martialed for disobedience and drummed out of the army. He was declared *"unfit to serve His Majesty in any military capacity whatsoever."*

Despite his military disgrace, Sackville remained politically active, especially because of his father's influence as Lord Lieutenant of Ireland. Sackville sat as a Member of both the Irish and British parliaments. In 1763 Sackville was appointed to the Privy Council and in 1769 became an ally of Frederick, Lord North, soon to become Prime Minister.

In 1770, as the result of a Will, Sackville became Lord George Germain. But while he might change his name, Sackville could not change his persona. Lord North appointed Sackville to his Cabinet in 1775 as Secretary of State, which placed Sackville as the Minister directly in charge of operations in the thirteen American colonies. Germain's arrogance and indolence contributed to British political and military missteps, helping make possible in no small way the disaster at Saratoga.

A confirmed "warhawk," Sackville was the only Cabinet member who desired to keep the American war going after the British capitulation at Yorktown. North's fall from power in 1782 brought

Sackville's retirement, though King George III rewarded him by granting the titles Baron Bolebrooke and Viscount Sackville of Drayton. Sackville died on 26 August 1785 at Stoneland Lodge, Withyham, Sussex.

### Frederick North (1732-1792)

Frederick North, known as Lord North of Kirtling, 2nd Earl of Guilford, was born in London on 13 April 1732, the son of a Tory nobleman, the 1st Earl of Guilford. Lord North was educated at Eton and Christ Church, Oxford. He was elected to Parliament at age 22 for Banbury, as his father was High Steward for that town. He remained a Member for Banbury for nearly forty years.

Lord North was made Paymaster-General in 1766 upon being sworn by the Privy Council. The next year, after the death of Charles Townshend, the Duke of Grafton appointed North to be Chancellor of the Exchequer. A solid Tory, North succeeded the Duke of Grafton as Prime Minister in March 1770. He retained his post as Chancellor of the Exchequer while serving as Prime Minister until his ouster in 1782.

North was amiable and conciliatory, and was thus able to maintain his majority in the Parliament despite the opposition of Edmund Burke, Lord Rockingham, and many other Whigs. King George III found him pliable and retained him in office, as the king was desperate to ward off the return of the "Rockingham Whigs" to power.

As Prime Minister – and pressed heavily by the king – Lord North found himself often in untenable positions. Indeed, from 1779 North had concluded that the war in America could not be won, yet the king (and others like Sackville) insisted that it be kept going. That said, Lord North was behind the Boston Port Bill of 1774, favored retaining the tax on tea, and initially supported punitive measures against the rebellious colonists. He thus is responsible in part for the onset of the American Revolution.

When the British surrender at Yorktown became known in London, the end of North's political career was in sight. Although Lord North survived a number of votes of "No Confidence," his majority finally broke in March 1782 when he introduced a bill asking for another large war loan. North's ministry collapsed and he went into retirement. His vision now failing, Lord North succeeded to his father's titles in 1790 and died in London on 5 August 1792.

### Charles Watson-Wentworth, Lord Rockingham (1730-1782)

Charles Watson-Wentworth, also known as Lord Rockingham, was born on 13 May 1730 in London, descended from two very distinguished families. In 1645 Charles I granted the title Baron Rockingham (a reference to the Watson family's castle Rockingham in Northamptonshire) to his grandfather. Rockingham was educated at Westminster and St. John's College, Cambridge. In 1751 he was appointed Lord Lieutenant of the East Ridings of Yorkshire, a position he held until 1763.

Politically a Whig, Lord Rockingham served as Prime Minister from July 1765 to July1766, succeeding George Grenville. He led a Whig ministry that reversed many of the Acts of Parliament that had unsettled the American colonists, notably the unpopular Stamp Act. Indeed, his ministry was popular in America and many colonists believed that conciliation with Great Britain was possible.

Rockingham's ministry fell in 1766 and was succeeded by the Duke of Grafton whose policies conformed somewhat more closely to the king's wishes. In turn, Grafton handed the Seals of Office as Prime Minister to Frederick, Lord North, in March 1770.

In Opposition, Rockingham and his supporters, including figures such as Burke, Fox, Barre, and Shelburne, advocated conciliation with the colonies and firmly opposed punitive actions. The Whigs stepped up their attacks on the war party in Parliament after shots were fired at Lexington in 1775, though their criticism of the war was somewhat muted after the signing of the Franco-American alliance.

With Lord North's fall in March 1782, Rockingham again found himself Prime Minister, though he died unexpectedly on 1 July at the age of 52. Edmund Burke, one of Rockingham's admirers, wrote his epitaph: *"A man worthy to be held in esteem, because he did not live for himself...He far exceeded all other statesmen in the art of drawing together...various dispositions and abilities of men, whom he assimilated to his character and associated in his labors."*

### James Moody (1744-1809)

James Moody, a staunch Tory Loyalist, was born in Little Egg Harbour, New Jersey, on 1 January 1744. A successful farmer with 500 acres and livestock, Moody lived in Sussex County not far from the Delaware River with his wife and children. Though a farmer, he had numerous Loyalist friends and contacts in many parts of New Jersey.

As the crisis in the Thirteen Colonies deepened, Moody did not hide the fact that he was a King's Man. This resulted in an attempt by Patriot militia in New Jersey to arrest Moody in April 1777. Moody and several Tory neighbors evaded this attempted arrest, marched to Bergen, New Jersey, and there enlisted in a Loyalist regiment. Shortly thereafter, James Moody became a recruiter and enrolled Tories from Sussex County and from Northampton County, Pennsylvania, into units supporting the Crown.

Not content to be a mere recruiter, Moody and his brother, John Moody, began to engage in partisan warfare in the areas of New Jersey and Pennsylvania familiar to them. The British soon recognized his abilities and Moody was commissioned an Ensign. General Knyphausen, deputy to Sir Henry Clinton, selected James Moody and his followers to kidnap or assassinate the Patriot governor of New Jersey. The plot miscarried and Moody was captured and imprisoned at West Point. Upon escaping from West Point, however, Moody returned to Sussex County and resumed his partisan activities.

In March 1781 Sir Henry Clinton decided to intercept the rebel mails and picked Ensign Moody for the job. Post Riders carried the public mail along set routes and at regular times in order to collect mail from the public or exchange mail with other Post Riders. Even so, snatching a mail pouch was a potentially dangerous business. Moody and his colleagues would have to cross through the American lines, avoid hostile patrols, hide somewhere near the post road, and often wait for hours in snow, rain, or cold weather for a Post Rider to appear. Despite the difficulties, Moody quite often succeeded in robbing the public mails and bringing his booty to British intelligence officers in New York. His most significant capture was the mail pouch taken after the Wethersfield conference.

Following the British defeat at Yorktown, Moody left New York for London in May 1782 in the company of General Clinton. His family joined him about a year later. His services to the Crown were not forgotten, and James Moody was granted an estate at Sissibou, Nova Scotia, and the permanent rank of Ensign. He died at Weymouth, Nova Scotia, on 6 April 1809.

# The French

### Admiral de Ternay (1723-1780)

Charles Henri Louis d'Arsac, Chevalier de Ternay, was born 27 January 1723, the son of Charles Francois d'Arsac, Marquis de Ternay, probably in Angers, France. He became a page to the Knights of Malta at age 14, and joined the French navy in 1738. Rising slowly through the ranks, de Ternay received his first ship command in 1761 and the following year slipped his squadron through the British blockade of Brest, landed on Newfoundland, and seized the fort at St. John's. In 1771 he became the equivalent of a Commodore and was given command of the Ile de France (today's Mauritius) and later Reunion. In 1776 he was promoted to Rear Admiral.

Admiral de Ternay was placed in command of the fleet designated to escort General Rochambeau's expeditionary corps to America in 1780. De Ternay sailed from Brest, France, on 15 April 1780 with seven ships-of-the-line, three frigates, two cutters, one corvette, and 35 transports or warships outfitted for carrying supplies. His mission was to carry Rochambeau's 6,000 troops, siege artillery, and supplies across the Atlantic and provide a naval screen to protect French land forces once they were ashore.

De Ternay's squadron entered Narragansett Bay, Newport, Rhode Island, on 10 July 1780 and Rochambeau's expeditionary corps began disembarking two days later. Given its small size compared to the Royal Navy's squadron of 13 ships-of-the-line at New York under Admirals Arbuthnot and Graves, de Ternay's fleet nevertheless proved valuable as a defensive force. De Ternay provided Washington with his professional advice that the shallow water off Sandy Hook and the superior strength of the Royal Navy squadron made a naval investment of British-held New York infeasible.

Admiral de Ternay died of a fever aboard ship in Newport on 15 December 1780 and was buried at Trinity Church with full honors. Chevalier des Touches [Admiral Destouches] succeeded de Ternay as naval commander until the arrival in May 1781 of the Count de Barras. De Ternay was made a Member of the Society of the Cincinnati posthumously for his pivotal service during the American Revolution.

### Count de Vergennes (1719-1787)

Charles Gravier, Comte de Vergennes, was born at Dijon on 20 December 1719 of a minor aristocratic family. Educated by the Jesuits, he entered the diplomatic service under his "uncle" M. Theodore de Chavigny. Vergennes served in Portugal and Germany, as French ambassador in Constantinople in 1755, and later in Sweden where he assisted King Gustavus III in his revolution of 1772 and aided the pro-French faction in taking power. A seasoned French ambassador, Vergennes was named Foreign Minister upon the accession of King Louis XVI in 1774.

Vergennes believed that France's interests were best served by maintaining friendly relations with Austria, by protecting Turkish territorial integrity, and by opposing Great Britain in Europe and abroad. The centerpiece of Vergennes' foreign policy was to re-establish the traditional balance of power that had been overthrown by the British triumph in the Seven Years War and subsequent Peace of Paris of 1763. Although cautious in his dealings with Britain in the early years of the American Revolution, Vergennes was persuaded to support the rebellious American colonists covertly in order to weaken his national enemy. After the declaration of war in 1778 Vergennes' skillful diplomacy prevented the British from finding a single European ally. Moreover, he persuaded Empress Catherine of Russia to form the League of Armed Neutrality in 1780 that effectively closed off northern Europe to Britain.

In addition to channeling covert assistance to the Americans through Beaumarchais, Count de Vergennes was instrumental in sending key European military professionals to assist Washington. Among these was Baron von Steuben who, during the terrible winter at Valley Forge, proved invaluable as the Continental Army's training master.

With the surrender of Lord Cornwallis and the dismantling of the British Empire in America, Count de Vergennes realized at least part of his foreign policy agenda. Despite this success, Vergennes' policies had led France to contract a staggering national debt that many historians hold as the trigger that ignited the French Revolution in 1789. The Count de Vergennes died at Versailles on 13 February 1787.

## Count de Rochambeau (1725-1807)

Jean-Baptiste Donatien de Vimeur, Comte de Rochambeau, born 1 July 1725 at Vendome, Loir-et-Cher, France, was originally trained to become a priest but then entered a cavalry regiment. During the War of the Austrian Succession (1740-1748) he served in Germany and rose to the rank of colonel in 1747. Rochambeau remained in service during the Seven Years War (1756-1763), was promoted to brigadier general in 1756 after distinguishing himself at Minorca, and made inspector of cavalry in 1761. In

1776 General Rochambeau was named governor of Villefranche-en-Roussillon.

A senior general by the outbreak of war with Great Britain in 1778, Count Rochambeau was placed in command of the French Expeditionary force sent to America in 1780. This force of 6,000 proved of great value in threatening New York and, in 1781, besieging Lord Cornwallis at Yorktown. After the Franco-American victory at Yorktown, Count Rochambeau remained in America, an honored guest, for another year before embarking for France in January 1783.

In recognizing Rochambeau's invaluable service in America, which helped bring about a favorable treaty of peace, King Louis XVI named Rochambeau commander at Calais and in Picardy, and later commander of Alsace. In the United States Rochambeau was named to the Society of the Cincinnati.

During the French Revolution, Count Rochambeau commanded the Army of the North in 1790-1791 when France was still a constitutional monarchy. He was created a Marshal of France in December 1791. Following the rise to power of the radicals and the Reign of Terror in 1793, Rochambeau was arrested and imprisoned and very narrowly escaped the guillotine. Upon his release in 1797, Rochambeau retired from public life.

Napoleon, an admirer of Rochambeau, granted him a pension for life. Rochambeau died at Thore-la-Rochette, France, on 10 May 1807.

## Count de Grasse (1722-1788)

Francois-Joseph-Paul, Comte de Grasse, was born at Le Bar-sur-Loup, France, not far from Toulon on 13 September 1722, and went to sea at age 12. De Grasse entered service in 1734 on the galleys of the Knights of Malta where he labored for six years. At age 18 in 1740, already a seasoned sailor, de Grasse joined the French navy as the War of the Austrian Succession (1740-1748) broke out.

In 1747 de Grasse was captured and remained a prisoner of war in England until the end of the war.

Upon his return to France, de Grasse was made a naval Lieutenant and served under the Marquis de La Galissoniere and later Admiral d'Ache in the East Indies during the Seven Years War (1756-1763.) Count de Grasse was promoted to naval Captain in January 1762 and received the brevet of a Knight of St. Louis in 1764.

With the signing of a treaty of alliance between France and the United States in February 1778, Great Britain declared war on France. De Grasse served as Captain of the "Robuste" under Admiral d'Orvilliers at the Battle of Ushant in July 1778. Promoted to the rank of Rear Admiral, he sailed from Brest in 1779 to the French West Indies in command of a squadron to join Count d'Estaing's fleet.

Returning to France, Count de Grasse was promoted to Admiral (lieutenant-général des armées navales) and sailed again from Brest for the West Indies on 24 March 1781. His fleet consisted of 23 ships-of-the-line and a large convoy. De Grasse arrived off Martinique 28 April 1781, and next day fought an engagement with the English fleet under Admiral Hood, which resulted in Hood's withdrawal. On 2 June 1781 he captured the Island of Tobago and then proceeded to Cape Français (now Cap Haïtien) where he found a French frigate bearing dispatches from Washington and Rochambeau urging his cooperation against British forces then stationed in Virginia. De Grasse acted without delay, sending back word of his planned arrival in Chesapeake Bay in August.

Naval historians consider the Second Battle of the Capes, fought in early September between the French fleet under Count de Grasse and the British fleet under Admiral Graves, to be one of the decisive naval engagements of history, as it sealed Lord Cornwallis' fate and spelled the end of British rule in America.

After playing a key role in the Franco-American victory at Yorktown, de Grasse sailed back to the West Indies. For a time he enjoyed success, but in April 1782 Admiral Sir George Rodney attacked de Grasse off Martinique. Known as the Battle of the

Saintes, the French and British fleets fought desperately from dawn to dusk, but the result was the utter destruction of the French fleet and capture of Count de Grasse.

Again a prisoner of the English, de Grasse returned to France after the conclusion of peace to face criticism at home. He demanded a court-martial which exonerated him of blame for the great defeat, but the "court of public opinion" dogged him to his death. He died, an embittered man, on 11 January 1788 at Paris.

### Gilbert du Motier, Marquis de Lafayette (1757-1834)

Better known by his title, Marquis de Lafayette (also spelled La Fayette), Marie Joseph Paul Yves Roch Gilbert du Motier was born into an ancient noble family on 6 September 1757 at Chavaniac, France. His father, a French soldier, was killed at the Battle of Minden in 1759. Lafayette aspired to be a soldier and, due to his noble birth, was accepted into the court of Louis XVI.

Lafayette was inspired by a desire to win glory, but also found himself caught up in the spirit of the American Revolution. Volunteering to serve without pay, Lafayette arrived in Philadelphia in July 1777 – only weeks before its fall to General Howe. He was only 19 when he joined Washington's army.

Lafayette fought with distinction at Brandywine on 11 September 1777, wintered with Washington and the Continental Army at Valley Forge, and emerged to fight a skillful retreat from Barren Hill in late May 1778.

In early 1779 Lafayette returned to France to speak with Count de Vergennes about the advisability of sending major land and naval forces to aid the Americans. He arrived back in America in April 1780, and the forces he had requested followed in July. These included the 6,000 French soldiers under Rochambeau and the squadron under de Ternay.

Not content with this contingent, Lafayette continued to importune his government for more assistance – in particular, a powerful French fleet capable of defeating the Royal Navy in American waters. Fluent in both French and English, Lafayette may be considered the "indispensable man" at the pivotal Hartford conference of September 1780 between Washington, Rochambeau, and de Ternay. After victory at Yorktown, the Marquis de Lafayette – still only 24 – was hailed as the "Hero of Two Worlds" and was promoted Brigadier General (marechal du camp) in 1782 by his king.

In 1789 Lafayette served as vice president of the Estates General and presented a draft of the Declaration of the Rights of Man. In addition, he served as head of the National Guard, and sought to ensure domestic order. With the rise to power of the radicals, Lafayette was imprisoned for five years until freed by Napoleon in 1797.

After Napoleon's fall, Lafayette served as a deputy in the French Assembly under the Bourbon kings, though he supported Louis-Philippe as constitutional monarch in 1830. Lafayette experienced a triumphal return to the United States in 1824, visiting all 24 states and receiving many honors. He died at Paris on 20 May 1834 and was buried at Picpus Cemetery under soil taken from Washington's grave at Mount Vernon.

### Chevalier de la Luzerne (1741-1791)

Anne-Cesar, Chevalier de la Luzerne, was born in 1741 in Paris to a noble family from Normandy that had holdings not far from Le Vey on the Carentan Peninsula. Anne-Cesar, a soldier and diplomat, had two older brothers who distinguished themselves: Count Cesar-Henri de la Luzerne, governor of the French colony of Sainte-Domingue and later naval minister, and Cesar-Guillaume who became a cardinal.

Anne-Cesar entered the French army during the Seven Years War (1756-1763) and by 1762 rose to the rank of Major General in command of the Royal Grenadiers.

After the war, Chevalier de la Luzerne entered the French diplomatic service and was appointed Minister to Bavaria. In 1779 the foreign minister, Vergennes, named de la Luzerne the second French minister to the United States government, then seated in Philadelphia (the British having withdrawn in 1778.) He remained in that position until 1784 when the Chevalier returned to France. King Louis XVI bestowed the Order of Malta on de la Luzerne in recognition of his diplomatic service in America. Chevalier de la Luzerne is said to have given unstinting support to the fledgling United States, even providing his personal funds to help feed the soldiers.

Washington thought highly of Chevalier de la Luzerne and in 1789 directed Thomas Jefferson, then Secretary of State, to write an official letter thanking de la Luzerne for his valuable wartime services. He was a member of the Society of the Cincinnati. The Chevalier de la Luzerne was appointed Ambassador to Great Britain, but died in London on 14 September 1791.

### Count de Barras (1719-1791)

Born in 1719, Jacques Melchior Saint-Laurent, better known as the Comte de Barras, was a French admiral who ably supported the French expeditionary force under Rochambeau in 1781, and later reinforced Count de Grasse at Chesapeake Bay.

The Count de Barras succeeded Admiral Destouches in May 1781 as commander of French naval forces at Newport, Rhode Island. Although some biographies give the impression that de Barras bucked the authority of the French supreme commander (the Count de Rochambeau) and give out that de Barras planned to attack Newfoundland instead of the British forces in Virginia, it is more likely that the admiral was fully aware of overall allied land and naval strategy, and placed himself without reservation under Rochambeau's command.

On 27 August 1781 Admiral de Barras sailed from Newport with eight ships carrying the vital French siege artillery bound for Chesapeake. He kept his small fleet well out to sea to avoid any possibility of interception by Thomas Graves' superior squadron. However, after Graves' defeat at the decisive Second Battle of the Capes, de Barras slipped his fleet into Chesapeake Bay on 10 September 1781 to deliver the siege artillery from its storage facility at Newport to the waiting French and American troops at Yorktown. De Barras was present at the ceremonies marking Lord Cornwallis' surrender on 19 October 1781.

After the victory at Yorktown, de Barras served under de Grasse in the West Indies. He led a successful expedition to seize the island of Montserrat early in 1782, and despite illness late in March 1782 in Martinique, was present with de Grasse at the pivotal Battle of the Saintes in April. This British naval victory destroyed French sea power in the West Indies and prevented a possible French attack on Jamaica and other British islands.

De Barras returned to France in 1783. He was promoted to Vice Admiral on 1 January 1791, when France was a constitutional monarchy, but died shortly thereafter.

# British Forces in Select Southern Areas

### British Forces in Select Southern Areas

| Date | State | Total | Comments | Source |
|---|---|---|---|---|
| 1 Aug 1780 | SC | 6,589 | 1,000 in Georgia, not counting 4,000 Loyalists | Sherman 7th ed. page 632 |
| 1 Dec 1780 | SC | 7,384 | Rein. by Leslie | Ibid. |
| 31 Dec 1780 | SC | 13,382 | 9,107 fit for duty, 2,000 in the field under Cornwallis, and 1,500 under Leslie; 2,000 to 3,000 garrisoning Camden, Ninety-Six and other posts | Ibid. |
| 1 May 1781 | NC | 1,435 | Under Cornwallis | Ibid. page 484 |
| 1 May 1781 | VA | 5,305 | Under Phillips and Arnold, inc. reinforcements enroute | Ibid. page 508 |

# British Forces in Select Southern Areas

| Date | State | Total | Comments | Source |
|---|---|---|---|---|
| 1 Aug 1780 | SC | 6,589 | 1,000 in Georgia, not counting 4,000 Loyalists | Sherman 7th ed. page 632 |
| 1 June 1781 | VA | 5,312 | Cornwallis took command of all British forces in Virginia with the death of Phillips, Arnold returned to NYC. Cornwallis should have had about 7,500 men. This difference may be accounted for by men under Leslie manning fortifications in Portsmouth and losses to sickness and desertion* | Ibid. pp 513-4 |

*According to Sherman 7th ed, page 531, by 10 June 1781 Wayne with his Pennsylvania Regiments joined Lafayette's Corps in Virginia bringing the total to around 4,500. By 19 June Lafayette's Corps had 2,000 Continentals and 3,200 Virginia militia and riflemen. Therefore Lafayette was gaining forces while Cornwallis was losing men. According to Sherman 7ed, page 506, In May/June 1781 a total of 7,854 Continentals mustered at Peekskill, West Point, and Virginia of which only 4,541 were fit for duty. This left the Americans far short of the numbers needed to attack NYC.

# G.L. LAMBORN

Larry is a retired U.S. Army Reserve full Colonel and CIA Senior Operations Officer with more than forty years (1967-2013) combined service to the American people, to include duty in Vietnam, Korea, Afghanistan, El Salvador, and many other Third World "hot spots."

He is a specialist in insurgency and revolutionary warfare and is author of "Arms of Little Value" (Casemate, 2012) and "Jihad of the Pen" (DIA, 2010.)

A SAR member, Larry is proud of his Pennsylvania and Virginia Revolutionary War ancestors and is a great admirer of George Washington. He holds a BA in History from Washington University (St. Louis,) an MA in Chinese Studies from the University of Washington (Seattle) and is an Air War College graduate.

He is also Past Commander and Life Member of American Legion Post 177 in Fairfax, Virginia, and a Sons of Norway member.

# W.L. SIMPSON, JR.

Bill is a retired U. S. Navy Lieutenant Commander with 20 years' service as a Surface Warfare Officer; a retired GS-13 Wargaming Specialist with 20 years government service at the Marine Corps Wargaming Division; and currently is a Senior Wargaming Specialist with the Center for Naval Analysis.

He has a BS in Geology from the University of South Carolina and a MS in Education from the University of Southern California.

An active member of the Virginia Society Sons of the American Revolution (VASSAR), he has held many local and state offices in VASSAR culminating with State President of the Virginia Society in 2009-2010.

As an SAR member, he became a popular speaker by giving interesting and well-prepared talks on Revolutionary War topics. For over 20 years he has, by invitation, given presentations to the Marine Corps War College, many Daughters, Sons, and Children of the American Revolution Chapters and other civic organizations. One of these presentations "The Great Deception" was the inspiration for this book.

www.whitehartpublications.com

www.ingramcontent.com/pod-product-compliance
Lightning Source LLC
Chambersburg PA
CBHW021436080526
44588CB00009B/547